Clint Adams is a former police officer who studied psychology and later, rehabilitation. Clint's police, injury management, senior HR roles and working with asylum seekers have made him develop insights into the psychology and social interactions of individuals in trying conditions. He has developed various behavioural and leadership programs to help people deal with various issues from PTSD to bullying and harassment.

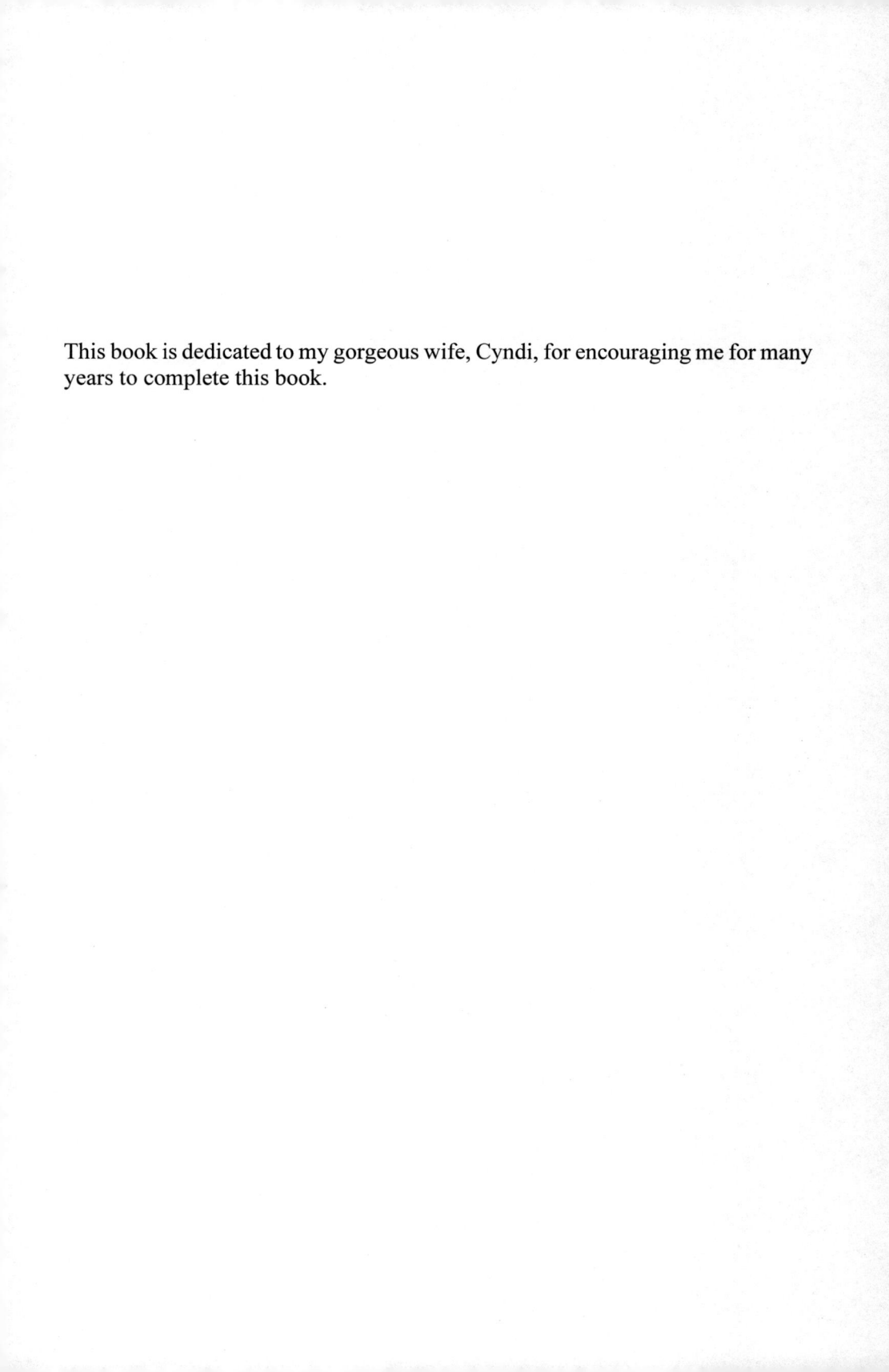

This book is dedicated to my gorgeous wife, Cyndi, for encouraging me for many years to complete this book.

Clint Adams

LIGHTING THE BLUE FLAME

AUSTIN MACAULEY PUBLISHERS™
LONDON * CAMBRIDGE * NEW YORK * SHARJAH

Copyright © Clint Adams (2020)

The right of Clint Adams to be identified as author of this work has been asserted by him in accordance with section 77 and 78 of the Copyright, Designs and Patents Act 1988.

All rights reserved. No part of this publication may be reproduced, stored in a retrieval system, or transmitted in any form or by any means, electronic, mechanical, photocopying, recording, or otherwise, without the prior permission of the publishers.

Any person who commits any unauthorised act in relation to this publication may be liable to criminal prosecution and civil claims for damages.

A CIP catalogue record for this title is available from the British Library.

ISBN 9781528913973 (Paperback)
ISBN 9781528960694 (ePub e-book)

www.austinmacauley.com

First Published (2020)
Austin Macauley Publishers Ltd
25 Canada Square
Canary Wharf
London
E14 5LQ

Note: Throughout the book there are links for which, if you have an electronic copy, you can simply click and it should open; however, if you have a printed copy, you will need a smart-phone and a scanning app to open the QR codes.

Chapter 1

Welcome to my last day! My mind has been spinning today; I'm all over the place. Since my latest run in with Steele Connors, who is a classic bully and loves to pick on little guys like me, I find myself reliving every embarrassing detail. I can stand the pain that he inflicts on me but the humiliation of being hung up on the fire extinguisher, while everyone in the corridor laughs at you is another painful present that just keeps giving and giving. No one has the guts or desire to want to get me down, so I hang there until I can tear my shirt and plummet to the ground with a thud to even more thunderous laughter from Steele and the others.

I'm finally home and sitting in my room, but I know I can't take this anymore. I've been thinking about how I want to end it for a few weeks now and more so in the last few days. I flip and flop in my head, fearful of actually following through and then also just hating myself and my life. I really don't want to be here anymore. I cry a lot; I get angry and then sad in seconds. I keep reliving the humiliating things which have happened to me at school, and the way my step-dad, Rick, treats me. Mum is so pre-occupied with her new baby, Georgia, my half-sister, (she always wanted a girl) that I'm like this irritation, and because of my crap relationship with Rick, she seems to have sided with the new family which means I feel very isolated even when I'm home.

Welcome to my last day. I am Joshua McKenzie, 16 years old, in my second last year of high school. What a joke school is, I'm not very good at school and they push me through because no one wants to fail me. I couldn't give a damn about how I perform there; I already know I won't be here to need a job, I checked out a while ago. I've always been the easy target, a bit different, attracted to alternative clothes, music and anything else that mainstream kids don't seem to have interest in. I have some interest in death, the "dark arts", reading things on the occult. I'm not sure if I started out like that or if the way I have been treated has pushed me that way. I guess you don't really think about how you become who you become and what has influenced your thoughts.

I can't really answer that now, but I can tell you what has influenced my thoughts to end my life. I fluctuate between an internal rage at the ones I blame for me feeling like this, and sadness for myself for not being able to do anything about it. Don't get me wrong, for a while I would fight back, but that meant they took it as a challenge and with my size, and my fighting technique of a wounded camel, it was quite brutal. Crying in front of girls you like and being beaten up and "dacked" (that's having your pants pulled down if you haven't had the wonderful pleasure of making your underwear readily available for viewing pleasure without your consent), are all humiliating experiences which add to my predicament.

So here I am sitting in my room feeling a little sorry for myself. I have been doing research and seriously thinking about what songs I want to send to certain people for different reasons. Some I hope will feel sad for what they did to me and others for what they didn't do. I keep thinking of the quote I read once, a Martin Luther King quote, "In the end, we will remember not the words of our enemies, but the silence of our friends."

I guess I do remember what my enemies have done and that has had an impact but knowing your friends or people you thought were your friends, or could be friends do nothing while these things happen to you, makes you feel pretty crap. I guess Martin Luther King was right; it probably hurts more because you start to question whether anyone really gives a damn about you. I used to question that, but it's happened that much that I am under no illusion that anyone cares if I checked out. I know Mum would have some degree of sadness but she would move on pretty quickly with Rick and Georgia.

I really don't have any friends anymore, I can understand why my ex friends don't interject when I'm being beaten up, because I know if they did, they would be next and it's self-preservation in the concrete jungle of school. Why would they get involved when the teachers know what's going on and they do nothing? I guess they were students like us, also scared not really trained to deal with this crap. No, that's not good enough! They are adults; they are who we are supposed to look up to. They are here to make an attempt to at least stop us getting to the point where we don't want to be around anymore.

It's one thing to not know but a very different one when you know and turn a blind eye. "Wilful Blindness" they call it, I read about this, it's like the "Bystander Effect", where everyone sees something happening, but no one is doing anything when they know they should be getting involved, so no one does anything and people die on the streets.

Here's me slowly dying every day, I even think with sadness and depression and listen to depressing music that make me focus on the bad and in some sick perverted kind of way it makes me feel good, like I can share painful experiences. I don't really know how to even explain that feeling, I suppose it's like people who harm themselves, because their lives are so messed up, it's the only way they get any kind of sensation anymore; it reminds me of the song by Eminem called *Stan*.

(Scan the QR code or hold down Ctrl and click the link)

http://www.youtube.com/watch?v=aSLZFdqwh7E

I have thought of shooting my tormenters but I can't really see myself killing anyone, I thought about it, even planned it and it's not really hard to get a gun. But I could never see myself walking into school and shooting someone point blank like that. There are too many variables, I have never held a gun and would guess, I would not be a great shooter. I don't want to shoot anyone who really had nothing to do with where I am. I suppose I could hunt down Steele and waste him, but I know I can't do that. I would freeze and that's not an option, unfortunately it's a stark realisation that when I look at me as a person, I'm pretty piss weak. This thought makes me feel like crap again, again the sadness and feeling sorry for myself overwhelms me.

I'm crying again. I focus on what's not good, I can't see past that, I decide to listen to something else and put on 30 Seconds to Mars, *Closer to the Edge*. I love this song, it reflects where I am right now and if you have seen the film clip, it's pretty cool. I listen to those kids talking through the clip and they all have a "sadness" I can actually see. I haven't discussed this with anyone so I'm not sure anyone else can see that. I'm in a sad place and maybe it takes one to know one, but those people in the clip seem sad and are on the verge of where I am. One guy says if it wasn't for music, he wouldn't be here, I don't even think that is enough for me. It's funny watching the clip, I still think the girl at the end who says, 'Some people pray, I turn on the radio' is hot, but she still looks sad. I identify with these people, even the little girl who wishes people could stop fighting, but realises that can't happen, I see the sadness and the sense of helplessness that is also a part of my life.

(Scan the QR code or hold down Ctrl and click the link)

http://www.youtube.com/watch?v=mLqHDhF-O28

I'm no dill, I know thinking like this harms me. I just don't have anywhere to turn to. I've been to psychiatrists and psychologists and I can't relate to any of them, they are usually these old people who have their perfect lives and wouldn't know anything about my situation. I'm supposed to tell them what is bothering me. I can only tell the same story so many times.

Hi, I'm Josh. I'm being bullied at school and everyone laughs about it, and no one does anything to help me. I'm weak as piss and even my stepdad hangs it on me and tells me to toughen up, it will be character building.

What a tool! I don't want any more character building. I don't want these negative experiences anymore. I want to be allowed to make friends, breeze through life laughing and smiling like everyone else, but that just doesn't happen. I can't really see any happiness or joy in my life.

I am consumed by my own negative thoughts and can't seem to break the pattern. I'm always scared at school and self-conscious around others. *Are they looking at me, talking about me, secretly laughing and judging me?* The pressure to not be humiliated or shamed is unbearable. I worry about things that "could" happen or happen again, because an array of things that have already happened to me have left me shamed. If you have never felt true shame and embarrassment, I highly recommend it, apparently, it's character building. If character building is driving someone into a deep dark hole of depression, then I have more character than I need for my short life. If doing this prevents one person from not having gone through the same crap I did, then I will be happy.

I never really noticed how things spiralled out of control for me, now I'm here and I don't really feel anything out of the ordinary. I still have that pit in my stomach like I just lost my wallet with my life savings in it or the same feeling when I asked Leah out and she laughed me off, I know she did it in a polite way but there was still a look of *Are you serious? What would make you think I would go out with you?* I don't even know if my perception of that event is true, I don't trust my thinking anymore. As I said, I'm all over the place.

Wow, I guess I really do let my thoughts take me to a bad place. I automatically think of all those events that tell me I'm not worthy. I'm a piece of crap and girls like Leah really are better than me. The scrawny body, the acne, the lack of any type of sporting ability whatsoever just seem to confirm this view of myself. I make ET look buff. Rick doesn't think much of me. Even my friends seem to stay away from me and don't really do anything to stop me getting the snot beaten out of me as some kind of daily ritual.

I find myself replaying events in my head and feeling a little sorry for myself. I cry a lot and then feel worse as I can't stand how pathetic I am. This makes me cry again and then I crack it with myself for being so pathetic. I recognise the cycle but I can't stop doing it. I see no other way out. The intensity, if you can call it that, of my sadness and depression is overwhelming me. I can't handle the pain in my stomach, the consistent adrenaline, I think it's that surge, some might call it extreme stress, I don't know.

I want to listen to something calming, I put on *Mountain* by Chocolate Starfish, it's a cool Aussie song, and even though it's a sort of power type ballad, it still manages to make me sad.

(Scan the QR code or hold down Ctrl and click the link)

http://www.youtube.com/watch?v=iGf4bQ7exMs

I think I'm looking for things to keep me in this state. My self-pity is driving me to look for things that take me and keep me in that mindset. I want to be free from this feeling. I really don't want to live like this, the final alternative is it for me. I worry now that I might be too damn gutless to even follow this through. *Can you believe that I can worry that I'm too scared to even kill myself?* Yet another thought which tells me I'm just not worthy to be here.

I start to think where did it all go wrong? I was a happy kid all through primary school, had friends, played soccer, genuinely enjoyed life with Mum and Dad and our dog. We lived in a nice quiet coastal town which was where I went to primary school. I loved the beach and we would go visit my parents' friends who also happened to have kids who I became friends with. I actually really liked their daughter, Emily, who was my age and we would hang out at school and do lots of things together. I always liked her and I certainly got the feeling that she liked me.

Things changed when my parents got divorced, my dad had an affair and Mum found out about it. He changed completely when she told him she knew. He got really angry with her and me and really just walked out and wanted nothing to do with us. I knew he moved in with the other woman and they moved interstate and he has had nothing to do with us since. I knew their split was not my fault, but I couldn't help but feel like crap when I would think how he could just distance himself from me so easily and not even give a damn enough to send me a card on my birthday.

When he moved out, he forced us to move house, as Mum couldn't afford to buy him out. The house was never the same anyway so we moved away and I went to a different primary school for a couple of years and we lost contact with Emily and her family. I slowly felt my life start to change and I didn't play sport anymore, I pretty much didn't really want to socialise and found I only had a couple of casual friends who were guys who were loners as well. We talked about general crap, nothing deep enough to call a true friendship.

My mum did it tough too, always crying, sometimes not getting up all day, I was forcing her to eat. She kept playing music that reinforced what she was going through. The song that she kept playing which summed up her divorce was Sharon O'Neill's *Danced in the Fire*:

(Scan the QR code or hold down Ctrl and click the link)

https://www.youtube.com/watch?v=rSBO9hX5CKY

She also played a lot of '80s' stuff which I think reminded her of Dad and probably has a lot to do with me liking '80s' music too. When I finally went to high school and saw Emily there, I thought things were going to change for the better, but they didn't. It had been a couple of crucial years and we had both changed a lot. She was definitely more mature than me, she looked hot and I was a dorky immature loner, so any thought of a reconnection with her was doomed.

Whatever glimmer of hope I had of impressing Emily was quashed when Steele Connors took it upon himself to tip chocolate milk down the back of my pants and then yell out that I had crapped myself. Again, those words of Martin Luther King rang in my ears when I saw Emily laughing at me along with everyone else in the lunchroom that day. I never tried to talk to her again after that. I think for me, this was that "Ralph" from the Simpsons moment, when you see when his heart breaks.

(Scan the QR code or hold down Ctrl and click the link)

https://www.youtube.com/watch?v=kDnimQCvHxk

I was truly shamed and humiliated in front of lots of people. Until that moment I just didn't feel very good about myself, but this was where I started feeling like I wanted to die. I replayed that moment in my head hundreds of times and all I could focus on was Emily laughing at me, which hurt the most. Yes, others laughing at me was not fun, but here was someone who was my friend, was close to me once, and yes, we changed, but it hurt me a lot.

Every year of high school had been more of the same, but even though I was humiliated a number of times and also had been physically abused by this guy and his friends, that time was the hardest, because I guess before that I had been OK. After that I really questioned my worthiness and desire to live. I noticed my other relationships started to deteriorate, even the casual friendships I had previously. I wasn't really involved anymore. I was ostracising myself because I kept asking why anyone would want to be friends with me. I chose to deliberately avoid forming friendships, because in my view this left me more vulnerable to being humiliated. I guess my thinking was that if I was humiliated and I didn't have friends, it was somehow easier to deal with than if I did and they reacted like Emily did.

I tried keeping my head down hoping Steele and his friends would get bored with picking on me, but they never did and here I sit. I take a large swig from the bottle of Jack Daniels I took from Rick's bar. I don't care that he would be angry because when he finds out, I will have left for good. I start to play *These Days* by Powderfinger because it reminds me of my chocolate milk incident because I played it a lot after that incident and it instantly makes me sad. The words resonate with me,

(Scan the QR code or hold down Ctrl and click the link)

https://www.youtube.com/watch?v=DpWVsOyf0n4

It's funny, it's like I want to feel sad, the song makes me sad, the melody, the words, but I want to play it again, it's hard to explain why I would want to keep myself sad. I guess it reinforces where I am, it's seems to justify all the crap going on and that I have somehow earned the right to feel sad whenever I want. I cry again.

I have had a few more shots of Rick's JD and feeling a little more "pumped". I'm really starting to feel it now and know I'm ready to go through with it. I pick the song my uncle mentioned to me many years ago that one of his friends chose for his funeral song, I think his name was Darren, my uncle was devastated but when he went and told me how they all celebrated his life afterwards, that's what I want. I want some recognition for me, nothing more. I deliberately sent some items to certain people for an effect when I am gone. I put on Darren's song which is long, while I get my things together. My rope, and tie it in a proper noos e, my chair and a few more swigs of JD. I already snail mailed the CDs to the right people so it's time to go. I put on the song again. *Fade to Black* by Metallica, the words resonate again with me, *"I have nothing more to give."* I'm not really scared, just sort of numb, sadness overwhelms me, no one has been there for me and no one is going to be there for me now. I loop the noose I kick the chair. *Fade to Black…*

(Scan the QR code or hold down Ctrl and click the link)

http://www.youtube.com/watch?v=wJ1QgQf3FFI

Chapter 2

My name is Steele Connors and I'm the guy a lot of guys want to be. I'm athletic, tall, good looking and everyone thinks I'm funny. I'm popular, have lots of friends and my parents are wealthy, so I get to buy and wear cool gear and do cool things. My grades are OK and while everything looks good on the surface, I'm not that happy. My dad is a bit of a control freak, he used to hit me when I was younger, a lot! I'm not sure if he hits my Mum but I suspect it. She always seems scared of him, they both drink excessively and they never really look like they have fun or care for each other. They very rarely go anywhere as a couple and when they do as a family it's to keep up appearances of "happy families".

My dad has always been hard on me; when I was in primary school, I got beaten up by this older boy who took my lunch money. When I went home crying and told my dad, he just told me to suck it up, stop whingeing and work on not letting it happen to me again. His view was, it's a dog-eat-dog world and you do what it takes to get to the top, you stand out from the crowd and take what you want in life.

Dad is successful, works for a large steel company and is the General Manager who worked his way up through the ranks. He is very intimidating and I admit it, I'm scared of him so I do what I can to keep on his good side. You don't dare question him, because he will just go berserk and believe me you don't want that happening too often. I don't think he's a very nice person and he certainly dominates both me and my older sister, Grace. He tells us what we must study and what we are going to do with our lives. I'm supposed to be an engineer because he can get me on some graduate program at work. I think he has our best interests at heart and wants us to do well, but our relationship with him is based on fear. Grace used to fight him consistently and challenge him, but a while ago she just gave up and pretty much does what he says.

She and I used to be close and talk about running away from home, but she changed and looks like she just goes through the motions now, she does what she's told, does her studies and nothing else. We hardly talk anymore and I have learnt from her not to take Dad on and challenge him. Mum does nothing to support us or protect us from him. We both don't respect her much at all. She's always out, comes home drunk and when she's not drunk, she is always stressed and anxious. She's very negative and a constant downer. Anyone that knows her avoids her because she whinges all the time and just sucks any enjoyment out of you while you talk to her. I don't think she has any friends, but I think that is all her own fault, even I avoid talking to her.

My relationship with her is superficial; we don't share anything of any substance. When I analyse my relationships, even those with my friends are a bit superficial. I don't really share my feelings with them. I think they hang out with me because it raises their profile. I'm not sure they think I'm all that great, but I am quite aggressive, funny and personable, so people do tend to hang out with me, because if they are on my good side, I tend to leave them alone. I do tend to tease and hang it on those who I don't consider friends of mine. I surprise myself how much I am like Dad in some ways.

There are some other kids at school that I pick on quite a bit, but everyone thinks they are dorks and they laugh when I play jokes on them. Like this weedy little dork Josh, I hung him up on the fire extinguisher the other day, and he was just hanging there while everyone laughed at him. I felt a little bad but then he is such a dork, he has no friends and everyone laughs and thinks it is funny when I do things to him. Even the teachers see me do it and let it slide so it can't be too bad. He even had the audacity to try to fight me a couple of times, who did he think he was? Of course it ended badly for him, but he never told on me and no one had a go at me for doing it, so it must be OK. Like my dad said it's a dog-eat-dog world. I'm lucky I'm the bigger dog and he is this pathetic individual. Can you believe he even cried in front of the girls in school a few times when I defended myself when he had a go, what a cry-baby!

I sometimes feel bad for him, because I remember when I got beaten up, but in all honesty, I actually feel good because I can dominate people like him, plus most of the other students don't seem to care too much about him, certainly no one stands up for him. Anyway, I don't think too much about him other than what I'm going to do to him next week. I go for things which have the most impact and at the time when most of the other students get to see it. My best work was when I poured chocolate milk down the back of his pants, and it looked like he shit himself. It was hilarious and everyone laughed, you should have seen his face, it was priceless. Again, he cried like a baby which only made everyone laugh even more. Man, people are ugly when they cry, he so brings the humiliation on himself.

Anyway, I'm in my room and I just love high-energy songs, I'm so into Flo Rida, I love *The Club Can't Handle Me*. I play it three times in a row, it gets me pumped!

(Scan the QR code or hold down Ctrl and click the link)

http://www.youtube.com/watch?v=NVRreyfxGGo

Chapter 3

My name is Emily Ross. I used to be that quiet girl who's very shy, I had guys interested in me, but I was so shy I didn't even really make eye contact with them. Then I went to high school and became friends with Emily Frost. I know, the name similarity was funny and made us instant friends. She was so much more confident than me and because of her I was introduced to the circle of popular girls. They referred to her as M1 and me as M2 for short. They determined who was in and who was out of the group. Steele Connors was definitely the hottest guy in our year level and all the girls thought so. I was shocked that he showed interest in me. It was good to be the one the other girls were envious of, as he was always flirting with me. He was charming, funny and definitely good looking. The only problem was that he was also having run-ins with an old family friend Josh, who I used to hang around with when I was younger, but then we lost contact when his parents divorced.

Emily and my other friends right from the start definitely made the call that Josh was "out" and I never really wanted them to think that we were friends. I agreed with them that he was a "dork", even though I felt sorry for him, I didn't want to jeopardise my standing in the group. I saw what it was like for those who were not "in" and I definitely did not want to be there. I'm not stupid, being in the "it" group may mean that others want to be part of your group and look to you for approval, but when you really think about it, it's not because they really like you, but more about what being included can do for them. All I know is that I made a conscious decision not to be associated with Josh, or go against the group's opinions too often about other students.

I guess you play a game to fit in, you tend to scan what everyone else in the group is saying and then assess what you actually say. I know I do this because I am worried if I stand up for someone who might be getting picked on or disagree with the group that they may not like me and I could end up on the outside. I feel accepted in this group even though some of the things they do to others are quite mean.

I even remember Steele picking on Josh one day when he put something in Josh's pants and yelled out to everyone that Josh had crapped himself. It was pretty funny and I remember laughing, but Josh looked right at me and when our eyes met, I could tell he was hurt by the situation and I felt really bad about it for him. I guess this is what they call cognitive dissonance, which I have been learning about in my psychology class. I know I justified my behaviour to myself by saying well he must deserve it or others wouldn't pick on him, and that if it was really bad surely others would step in and stop this stuff. I know teachers have seen this sort of stuff and do nothing about it, so I guess they figure it's just practical jokes. I don't know how convincing I am to myself but I still feel bad about these instances, because I know Josh has had a bad time of it and his parents' divorce wasn't easy for him.

I'm home and just thinking about all these things and to distract myself I put on one of my favourite songs. Chris Brown is sooo hot, I put his song *Yeah* X 3.

(Scan the QR code or hold down Ctrl and click the link)

http://www.youtube.com/watch?v=3mC2ixOAivA

The song gets me excited and I'm starting to feel good again, I do notice I fluctuate between feeling bad because of seeing Josh's face and the look he gave me and then trying to justify me laughing and also looking away. I get this pit in my stomach, because I know I let him down, I guess he was looking to me for some sort of support even though we really haven't spoken much since he started at this school. I know he tried to talk to me a few times but being honest with myself I deliberately avoided him and I guess he was able to realise that I didn't really want to reconnect and eventually stopped trying. Looking back, I was not really comfortable telling him to his face that I didn't want to be associated with him and that he should leave me alone because being associated with him would hurt my chances of being in the "it" group.

I had been struggling to find my way, my self-esteem was only OK but I was painfully shy and meeting Emily had changed all that, I was suddenly popular and my confidence was on the way up, it was too early and too big a risk to even acknowledge Josh as someone that was and would continue to be a friend of mine. Inside I feel horrible about what he would be thinking of me. I really don't like making anyone feel bad. I pretend when I'm with my friends that he is a dork and laugh at him, but I feel like crap when I'm by myself and think about it. It's this pain in my stomach I'm torn between wanting to not piss off my new group of friends and say to them to leave Josh alone. Steele also complicates things for me because I like the attention from him, he's cute and all the girls like him, and because he is interested in me it's an ego boost when others say how lucky I am that he wants to hang with me, but he picks on Josh and that does complicate things.

I can't think about him though, it's survival for me and I must be a bit selfish about that. I do have a soft spot for him, but I can't help the fact that he turned into a bit of a dork, which actually leaves him wide open to ridicule, he always wears black, is so scrawny and tends to wear '80s' gear like he's stuck in a time warp. He's no good at sport, hangs out by himself which means no one else thinks he's worth talking to, which just confirms to me that I should just focus on me and let him fend for himself and not get involved. Getting involved and saying something is fraught with danger for me, much more risky than if I just ignored it and did nothing. I still have a pit in my stomach when I think about it, though I guess I wish they would leave him alone, but I resign myself to the fact that there is nothing I can do.

So I check out a cool clip sent by Emily Frost to check out a wonder dog and mushy cute too.

(Scan the QR code or hold down Ctrl and click the link)

http://www.youtube.com/watch?v=fLclGPr7fj4

    The clip is cool and it takes my mind off Josh thinking and I start to think about Steele, hopeful he might call me to ask me out this weekend. I lie in bed thinking of my dad in Afghanistan and listening to a song that makes me think of him.
Fort Minor's *Where'd You Go*:

(Scan the QR code or hold down Ctrl and click the link)

http://www.youtube.com/watch?v=zQdglLeGQXM

    The song makes me sad and I cry because I miss him. The house is not the same without him here, he really sets the house alight and everyone feels good when he's around. My mum misses him too and she and I fight a lot when he's away. He seems to be the glue that binds the family, so when he's away it's like our lives go into limbo until he comes back. I actually welcome the feeling of sadness it's like it makes me feel closer to my dad somehow. It is hard to explain, but the song inspires a pain and the pain somehow makes me feel closer to him, like it connects us and he can feel that, so it connects us despite how far apart we are. It's crazy but I believe he will "feel" me and that makes me feel better but still sad. Weird huh? I drift off to sleep looking forward to him coming home in a few weeks.

Chapter 4

My name is Vicki Shaw, formerly Vicki McKenzie, I have a son, Joshua, from my first marriage and a daughter, Georgia, from my second marriage to my current husband, Rick. My first husband had an affair and when I caught him out, he walked out on me and Josh and for a while there I was in a very bad place. It was tough on Josh too, as he had to look after me and he showed strength a child shouldn't have to. It did take its toll on him and it was hard when we had to move from the family house and he had to change schools.

As I said, I was in a bad place, I started to question what I did or didn't do in the relationship that would have my husband of 16 years and partner of 18 years cheat on me and destroy what we had, or in my case thought we had. The other part that made me question myself and was probably the hardest part for me to deal with, was the fact that when I caught him, he could leave me and Josh behind so easily. Looking back, I was selfish through this, as I was so focused on what I had lost and how it affected me that I really didn't support Josh at all.

I remember fluctuating between absolute anger and inconsolable sadness. I would go days without wanting to get up. I lost lots of weight, wouldn't look after myself, eating and showering were things I suddenly started dodging. Josh would clean the house, look after himself and then clean me up and try to get food into me. I hardly acknowledged him, certainly showed him no mind, I was so absorbed in my own pain. I was in a lot of pain, crying so much I ran out of tears and tissues, I would just beat myself up asking why, hating myself, blaming myself. The personal shame I felt and the humiliation meant that I just couldn't face anyone, even those offering me help, and I just didn't want them near me. I would have been awful, I know I yelled and screamed at my friends and told them to leave me alone, some persisted, but like the show *Survivor* I outlasted them and "won". This drove all support away except for Josh.

If I had my time over, I would have done things differently. I resented my husband so much, but I also resented myself and it's not a good thing when you really hate…YOU. I was constantly thinking what if I had done this or that or showed him more affection or not have been so demanding or whingeing, it was awful. I was so tough on myself. I also made a mistake in trying to make contact with him again but he had obviously moved on before I even caught him. I was this irritant to him, which made it even more difficult to swallow. I even tried to use Josh as some kind of emotional blackmail, but he wanted a new life and it didn't include me or Josh. I then spiralled into another bout of self-pity and self-loathing, questioning how he could so easily let me and Josh go. It was a crashing realisation of how big a gulf there was between my view of our relationship and his.

I was on medication for depression and was getting counselling which didn't help me all that much but it did break the downward spiral and I was starting to at least look after myself, regular showers and eating crept back and I was starting to notice Josh again after a few months. I started reading self-help books and this allowed me to change how I was thinking. I reconnected with a couple of friends who kept hanging around despite my desire to be left alone and eventually the tide turned. I found that my anger towards myself started to turn its attention to my husband and this actually fuelled the change that was required. Don't get me wrong, it was not an instant change, I still fluctuated between the two but slowly but surely eventually the anger towards him became increasingly more while my self-hate became progressively less.

At the time, as I was going through it all, it was so painful and I just couldn't see it ending. Taking my own life entered my mind a number of times, but my fear of death was too great. I'd like to think I was too strong for that or that my love of Josh or something else was what prevented me from doing that, but in the privacy of my own thoughts, I know the truth. Fear of death is a sobering thought in itself and thinking back about those moments snaps me back to the present.

Back in my car, Georgia is sleeping in her car seat behind me after a big eventful day at day-care. She's such a little angel, she and Rick, my current husband, have been absolute blessings since my divorce and subsequent meltdown. I worry about Josh though, the break up was tough on him even though he didn't really react like I did. I suppose he was worried about me. I had freaked out and he stepped up and looked after me. When I finally came back from that dark place, a lot of time had elapsed from when his dad left us and he seemed to just get on with it. We moved, he changed schools and he seemed relatively unaffected, but he had been a very happy child with lots of energy and a positive outlook on life. He would play with his superhero toys and make up stories of heroic acts, he had such imagination and a certain sparkle. But since his dad left, he seems to have lacked that, I can't recall him actually "playing" since then.

I put it down to "growing up" his dad's departure brought that on a lot sooner, but there is more to it. He seemed OK when he moved schools and the next couple of years was OK even though he wasn't himself he didn't show anything negative that brought any concern into the equation. When he went to high school though, that changed. He started getting into fights at school, his grades started to suffer and he would fight with Rick a lot. He seemed very angry and would go into rages and we had concerns for him. I sent him to a few different counsellors, psychiatrists and psychologists, but he never really shared anything with them, I guess because we were forcing him to go to the sessions against his will, so nothing ever came of them.

He seems to be distancing himself more and more from me, I hardly see him come out of his room when he is home. He and Rick seem to have come to this agreement that they don't fight anymore, unfortunately that also means they hardly interact at all, which is not good. I really don't know what to do anymore. I spoke to the principal of his school and they don't seem to have any answers on what I can do. I try to talk to Josh, but he just shuts me out so I'm not even sure of what is going on. I suspect he might be getting bullied at school, but he doesn't complain about anything, he seems to deal with these things in a private way, the same as he did when his dad left. I still worry though. A Pink song comes on the radio and cuts the thread of my thoughts and I'm singing *Blow Me One Last Kiss*:

(Scan the QR code or hold down Ctrl and click the link)

http://www.youtube.com/watch?v=3jNlIGDRkvQ

I pull into the driveway and am a little surprised how dark the house is, obviously Rick's not home yet, which is no surprise, but Josh usually comes straight home from school and usually turns lights on in every room he enters. He doesn't have any extracurricular activities, so it is surprising that he is not home yet. I go inside with Georgia now half-awake in my arms and turn on the lights, I hear music from Josh's room, and assume he left it on accidently, but then I was last to leave and there was none on when I left so he must have come home and left again. It doesn't concern me too much, but I walk down the hall to his room to turn the music off.

I open his bedroom and there he is hanging from the exposed beam. It takes a few seconds for things to register in terms of what I'm looking at. I surprise myself by how long it takes for me to truly comprehend what I'm seeing. He is completely blue in the face. I see the chair overturned on the ground and I rush to pick it up and put it under him and try to take his weight off the noose, but I fall and have to do it again. I try a number of times and call for help repeatedly and am forced to run to the kitchen to get a knife and cut him down.

The next couple of hours is a blur of phone calls to 000, me doing some weird version of CPR and the ambulance arriving. I stand there watching them work on him, but all the while knowing he is gone and that I should have seen this coming. The feelings of my first husband leaving start to flood back, the feeling is truly gut wrenching, I am in some surreal world, it's like I'm there but I'm not. It's really hard to explain, but when your world just turns on its head and you have life-changing things happen, it's like everything just slows down and you are almost out of your own body, watching someone else experience the feelings, because I am numb. I catch myself thinking this and for some weird reason think of songs that remind me of feeling numb. I'm thinking Linkin Park and go into a safe place in my head I don't want to face this, it's crashing on me and I can't react to this with anything normal, it's nothing it is numb.

Numb:

(Scan the QR code or hold down Ctrl and click the link)

http://www.youtube.com/watch?v=kXYiU_JCYtU

The next few hours are really a new experience for me, even when my first husband left, I was able to take it in, decipher it and react. In this case I am really unable to feel anything, numbness is the best way to describe it. I'm not sad, highly emotional, shamed, nothing. I watched them take Josh away, I kept thinking I have to pack some clothes for him and went into some bizarre autopilot mother reaction to make sure he had clean underwear and warm clothes like he was going on school camp. I didn't actually pack those things but my natural instinct was to do that. Once he had left and it was just me and Rick, I didn't know what to do with myself.

I sit there and think about what just transpired and I can't help it, but I vomit on my rug and begin to clean it up immediately. Rick tries to help, but I scream at him to let me do it and to PLEASE leave me alone. He detects my emphasis and leaves me. I sit there and look at my discharge on the rug and I start to cry. It suddenly hits me like a ton of bricks. The sadness is like nothing I have ever experienced. I vomit again and keep doing so until nothing is left to come up. I dry retch again and again and my throat just starts to hurt. I sit there looking at it and don't know what to do. It is the single worst moment of my life, so many questions rush through my head. So many heavy and I mean HEAVY realisations start to hit home.

The police ask me lots of questions. I guess they have to treat it like a homicide. It's not until they ask if Josh left a note that I even think about going to his room since I found him. We all go to his room and look around and there sitting on his desk is a letter addressed to me. I open it nervously and Josh wrote:

Mum, if you are reading this, then I actually had the courage to go through with it and end my pain. I know that you love me and that this will be a sad event for you, but you need to know that for a long time now I have hated life. I have been thinking about ending it for a long time. I have felt worthless, humiliated and shamed and really been doing it alone. I know you have asked me how things were going, but I have never felt like talking about this. I found out early on at high school that bringing up that I was being bullied was actually worse for me. I got caught having a fight with a bully and when a teacher found us, they sided with him, because he was a good student, pretty boy and he sweet-talked them and even though I managed to convince them it was not my fault, nothing really happened to him and that just meant he targeted me even more.

I never told you because I know you would have gone down to the school and tried to get the bully in trouble, but the school is such a toothless tiger he would have got yard duty or detention or at best some kind of suspension, but his parents are rich and money talks. This would have meant even more pain for me, so I just tolerated it and fought back every now and then, but that also meant they worked harder on me, so I got to the point where I would just not react to anything they did to me, I would go into a "numb" zone and they could do their worst and I wouldn't let it get to me. I guess I just gave up on life and there was no enjoyment in it for me. Each day was just a worry for me and the anticipation of something negative happening became unbearable, I suppose you could say I was suffering from severe anxiety. You probably didn't know, but I would be physically sick almost every day before I went to school.

I'm not trying to make you feel bad, but I knew that I couldn't rely on you to be strong enough for me. The way you reacted when Dad left us was an eye-opener for me and I knew I needed to keep things from you for your own good. I don't know if you ever noticed how Dad leaving us affected me. I had to be strong for both of us because you just flipped out and it's funny to say this but I worried that you would do something bad to yourself and yet here I sit writing this to you.

I know you will move on as you have Georgia and Rick and I wish you all the best. I think you are better off without me there. I'm that boil on the arse cheek of your new family. I want you to do something for me and that is to get on with your life, I want you to dig deep inside and not let this get you the way Dad leaving did. I also have a request that if you do hear from Dad that it is my choice to not have him at my funeral. I blame a large portion of my unhappiness on him. His choices turned our worlds upside down and I cannot forgive him for that and then just walking out on us without ever peeking back.

I have some requests for my funeral. I want to be cremated and I have a list of songs I want played. The first is an old '80s' song by Time Bandits, which I chose because it reminds me of a time when we were a happy family and when we went on a holiday around Australia and in the clip the band themselves are doing the same thing and it's a tune that always sticks in my head. I loved the Big Pineapple and The Big Banana in Coffs Harbour. I remember a place called "Whoopie" near Coffs which was my favourite beach anywhere because the water was so warm and we would body surf all day. I also choose this song because I really don't know what happens to me when I end it. I'm not really religious and if there is a god, I'm pretty sure that suicides are frowned upon in heaven, so I'm double screwed either way so please play my songs, will you? Sorry the reason I chose this is I try to contort the message in my head so that I'm on an Endless Road and we just keep going in some shape or form, I wouldn't say I believe that it's just a thought.

Endless Road:

(Scan the QR code or hold down Ctrl and click the link)

https://www.youtube.com/watch?v=KIv6FYJkeVw&list=RDKIv6FYJkeVw#t=8

The next song I want played is by Powderfinger, which I chose because it sums up how I have been feeling for a long time, things never turned out like I had planned. I had no control over all events and the tone of the song is melancholy which was where I have been, and in some weird way has been what I have been attracted to. I feel like it is my fate to do this, like it's a morbid message I can send to help others.

(Scan the QR code or hold down Ctrl and click the link)

https://www.youtube.com/watch?v=DpWVsOyf0n4

My next choice is another older song from the 90s I think, called *Painless* by Baby Animals. I pick this because it's what I crave as I'm writing, which is to be painless, I can't stand my life and the pain. It's tough for a kid to take when your dad just walks out on you and doesn't even bother to want to make contact with you again and the person who should be helping you is a blubbering mess. The funny thing is Dad loved this song, he used to think the lead singer was hot and as a young boy I did too.

Painless:

(Scan the QR code or hold down Ctrl and click the link)

https://www.youtube.com/watch?v=4DRg7jK-_RA

Finally, I want a positive song called *Titanium*. I choose this because I wish I was this person, she sings that the bullets being fired at her just ricochet, and while she is being shot down, she has an inner-strength and won't fall. It's a song saying, I can take whatever you can give me and still get up. I want this to be my message and a destination for others like me, hopefully they won't fall like I have, unfortunately I'm not bulletproof.

Titanium:

(Scan the QR code or hold down Ctrl and click the link)

http://www.youtube.com/watch?v=JRfuAukYTKg

When I think of how I have been bullied, it's like they shoot bullets at you and you can do two things to stop the harm and that is to make the target bulletproof and even better to stop someone shooting them. You don't need a bulletproof vest if no one ever shoots at you! I don't know the answer. I don't know what people get out of making others hurt so much they eventually want to kill themselves? The fact that it is so prevalent scares me. I looked up statistics on bullying and it is alarming. The question is, if so many are being bullied, why is nothing being done and why don't they have some movement to rally the bullied to do something? I guess that is a question for someone else to answer not some dead kid.

Mum, I want you to be strong through this and take care of Georgia. At least you have Rick to support you. I know he and I never got on, but I know that was mainly my fault, I was angry with Dad and it transferred to Rick, I never really wanted a substitute and Rick was trying to get in, but to some degree I was bulletproof, I would never let him in and our relationship was doomed. Anyway, I know you guys can *make it, he is good to you and you deserve good things. I know you will be better off without me. I want you to play a song just for you and me, not at my funeral but by yourself and think of me when I was a happier kid. Please think of me on my birthday and enjoy the song. You know why I chose this for you and me. Josh.*

U2 *With or Without You*:

(Scan the QR code or hold down Ctrl and click the link)

https://www.youtube.com/watch?v=ujNeHIo7oTE

I sit and stare at the letter unaware of the tears streaming down my face. I know why he chose that song, it was always my favourite and whenever it would come on, the volume went up and we would sing at the top of our lungs. It always made me feel good to hear it, sing it and even now as I listen to it, it connects me with my baby boy, but there are tears now. It's bittersweet to hear it, and as much as I love the song, it has a slightly haunting feel to it and it definitely has a "pained" lyric I had never considered until now. I just loved singing loudly to it especially at the end when Bono is singing.

The police take the letter as it needs to be fingerprinted to verify Josh wrote it. Rick calls my parents and does the communications out to those who need to know. I fleetingly think about my ex-husband and as much as I believe he needs to know; I also want to respect Josh's wishes. I debate with myself for a while, but make my decision not to call when I realise, I only want him to know so that I can blame him for doing what he did, so I realise the reasons are selfish. I now have to go about organising the funeral.

I meet with the people from the funeral home and organise the music Josh requested. They ask me to pick out photos or video footage that summed up Josh's life and they will put it together with the music and make some kind of slide show to play during the service. They ask about favourite poems and verses from the Bible, I'm in a bit of a daze and pick things I'm not even sure of. I go home and start looking through photos and watch old home movies and this activity drives my thoughts to the end of the movie *Philadelphia* when Tom Hanks dies and everyone is watching an old film of him as a child playing on the beach to a Neil Young song. It's a very sad moment and so is what I'm doing, it's nostalgic and is weird to describe because it is good to remember good times, but sad at the same time because it will never happen again with Josh. I look it up on YouTube and am surprised to know that the song is actually called Philadelphia and listening to it again and watching the clip makes me cry uncontrollably.

Philadelphia end:

(Scan the QR code or hold down Ctrl and click the link)

https://www.youtube.com/watch?v=eks9GPnyJV0

    The words of the song are beautiful. I'm listening for some kind of meaning in everything at the moment, I guess my focus is different at present, I'm in a very different headspace to when Josh's dad left. His letter has forced me to be stronger, that if I'm not I would be letting him down again so I can't let that happen, I'm determined for that not to happen. But it's not easy, I still cry it was never an option not to.

Chapter 5

It's Saturday morning and I hear the doorbell go, Mum's up and I can hear her high heels on the floorboards as she walks to the door. I can hear her voice but can't make out what is actually being said. Then I hear her call me. I get up and walk to her and she says, 'Steele, a package arrived for you, I signed for it.' She hands me an express post envelope with my name on the front and the sender surprises me, it says Joshua McKenzie. I go to open it and then I'm suddenly suspicious, I haven't exactly been nice to this dweeb, I've made him cry a few times and he has tried to throw things at me, so I take a bit of care to see if there is anything sinister in the package. I carefully open it and find a CD in it with a post-it note stuck on it, that says, 'I'm a DVD play me you TOOL!'

I have a DVD Player in my room so I pop it in and there is Josh looking at me on the screen. He looks a bit tired and starts to talk, reading a letter which is in the package:

Well, hello, Connors, if you are watching this then I am dead. I have taken my own life and you have played a significant part in me doing that. I can't put all the blame on you, I know that, but you haven't made my life very enjoyable. In some weird way I have to give you some credit for your ingenuity on some of the stunts you pulled on me. I wouldn't have thought you were that smart, I always thought you were so stupid, that you thought Microsoft was a sexual dysfunction, ha. That's a Josh original not all that funny but then I'm about to kill myself so not really excellent conditions for humour.

I'm not here to beat you up, I actually am hoping that I can have some influence over what you do to other guys like me in the future, so that you can realise how hurtful those "jokes" are to a person. The embarrassment and shame can be unbearable. People laughing and ridiculing you is not good for the self-esteem. I would go home many times after your "events" and just want to end it. I thought of ways I could get you back. Killing you crossed my mind a few times. I thought of murder suicide as well. I built up a deep resentment towards you and even as I'm speaking here, I am still considering whether you even deserve to be here.

I have my reasons for not wanting to do that and I guess everyone deserves a second chance, so I'm sending you this with the hope that you don't do this to anyone else. I have sent other DVDs to other people and if you don't change your behaviour, they have instructions to send another DVD to the police where I blame you for me killing myself. It might not stick, but it might make life a little uncomfortable for you.

This is an opportunity for you to do the right thing and turn things around. I read about why bullies bully and one of the big factors are people who have been bullied themselves. I am not sure why you do but I ask that you ask yourself some honest questions. I know you probably don't give a shit about me and might even get some pleasure out of me being dead, but I can't do nothing, and this is my way to try to influence you. I have included some YouTube Clips for you to have a look at.

The first is about a kid who is getting bullied and then finally snaps. The bully gets hurt badly; the rest of the clip shows how much support is for the person being bullied. I wish I was big and strong enough to smash you on the ground like he did. I totally understand how this kid was feeling, I also lost my friends and my life hasn't had too many good days lately.

(Scan the QR code or hold down Ctrl and click the link)

http://www.youtube.com/watch?feature=endscreen&v=I_BdAk7H6Lk&NR=1

The second clip is the bully being interviewed, this person is YOU, and the only difference is you are bigger and stronger than me. You don't realise you have power and influence at school, no one wants to say anything against you or disagree with you, but behind your back no one really likes you and no one will admit to it. They are driven by fear; you are not really well liked. In this clip you can see how badly it affects this kid and even his father. You will also see how many people show support for the bullied boy and if I was big enough and was able to slam you on the ground like that, they would be supporting me.

(Scan the QR code or hold down Ctrl and click the link)

http://www.youtube.com/watch?v=__IjcLVBBYc

The thing I can't figure out is why lots of people laugh about this, obviously the bullies' friends are filming this and egging him on. I don't know what the bully gets out of it or what you get out of it when you do it. Maybe you have some issues yourself and this makes you feel like a big man. I guess that's the reason I think you deserve the chance to redeem yourself, because it is a complicated system of events. I don't actually know why you ever started picking on me, only you can answer that. The next clip is the song *How to Save a Life*. I chose this because I want you to know that you have contributed to my death, but you can contribute to saving a life by stopping what you have been doing and with your influence and power at school you can actually do something to stop others doing the same. I want to think that I'm changing things here and this is the way I can do that. Me dying can do more good than me living, how crap is that? But it's true. *How to Save a Life*:

(Scan the QR code or hold down Ctrl and click the link)

http://www.youtube.com/watch?v=cjVQ36NhbMk

The final one is about a girl who also dies because of being bullied. Have a look at her as you watch the clip, she is a gorgeous girl and now her family is missing a big part of their lives because tools like you think it's funny, because I guess it makes you feel more significant. Forgive me if I sound a bit condescending, even a turd like you should be able to detect the sarcasm in my voice. I think I've had enough to say to you. I hope I can come back and haunt you. Do something better you have a second chance. I don't!!! She was bullied to death:

(Scan the QR code or hold down Ctrl and click the link)

http://www.youtube.com/watch?v=2vAMxKvZqwU&feature=fvwrel

The DVD ends and I follow the links he gave me. I don't really know what to think. It enters my mind that this is some stunt, like I'm being Punk'd or something. Still it's pretty gutsy of him because if this is his version of a joke, I guarantee he won't be laughing Monday. I decide to do some kind of investigation and ride past his house on my bike. There are a few cars out the front, so I wait to see if anyone comes out, I listen to my music as I wait, and after 30 minutes or so a couple emerge, an older lady with grey hair and she is clearly upset as she is wiping her nose with a tissue and being consoled by a chubby older dude. Josh's dad, I'm guessing here, comes out and he looks a pretty down, it's hard to say but there is certainly more in the body language that makes me think he might have done it.

My stomach starts to turn, I'm worried now, I guess the worry is a combination of things, self-preservation, he did say he sent information to someone else about what I did, and also the fact that I really didn't want him dead. I try to convince myself that maybe he didn't get the job done, because he was alive when he made the DVD and all I saw was some people leave the house a bit sad. I don't know what to think.

I go home and get online to see if anyone on Facebook might know anything, but no one has put anything on. I don't want to put anything on either because if it is a joke I look like a tool. I guess I have to wait, so I watch the DVD again and analyse his face and body language more intensely. He definitely looks like he is tired or stressed as he looks very withdrawn. I pick up a slurring of his words, it's only slight but it's there. I also see behind him on a chest of drawers is a bottle of

Jack Daniels and only a partial view of a glass, so I suspect he has been drinking. Towards the end you can see the emotion start to get to him when he yells, 'But I don't!!!' and then there is about another two seconds of footage as he walks to the camera to turn it off, his face is close to tears and I think he is about to wipe away tears before the screen goes black.

I'm starting to get a nagging feeling that Josh may have done what he said in the film. I start to think about what that means for me. The fact that he sent me the DVD clearly shows where he sees the responsibility for how he is feeling. I guess I have been pretty mean to him, physically through actual assaults, nothing too bad though, and then also through embarrassing him in public. I can understand that he wouldn't like me, I never really liked him, but then I never really disliked him either. The more I think about it, I did those things to get a reaction from others, the stunts I pulled always got laughs and he was one of the easiest to do things to. I suppose no one really hung out with him so he didn't have anyone backing him up, so it made him easier to pick on. I don't remember it being deliberate. He just stood out as a dweeb and once I started on him people started to laugh. I suppose I am a funny guy and a bit of a "show pony" but getting him to the point where he would kill himself is not something I wanted or even thought about.

Yes, he got upset with me a few times but never showed the level of distress or depression that would give me any insight that this was coming. It's a weird feeling that you could be responsible for the death of someone. I start to feel a bit sick and my head starts to spin. I'm whipping myself into a frenzy in my head and I have to tell myself that it's not confirmed that he may have set the whole thing up and been watching me and I end up on YouTube with me outside his house watching some old people whose cat had died or actors he knows. This doesn't help so I put on some music to make me feel better. I put on a Matchbox '20s song, *she's so Mean*:

(Scan the QR code or hold down Ctrl and click the link)

https://www.youtube.com/watch?v=-8WLa6umgdw

I start to feel a bit better and then just check out random stuff on YouTube and I find this and have a bit of a giggle.
Fox hat:

(Scan the QR code or hold down Ctrl and click the link)

http://www.youtube.com/watch?v=uTjC-atS0iE

Chapter 6

I hear a knock at the door and I leave Emily waiting on my room phone to answer it, Mum is out. At the door is a courier who says, 'Package for Emily Ross.'
I answer, 'That's me.' I'm a little surprised to even receive a package. It's an envelope addressed to me and the sender's name is a bit of a surprise, Joshua McKenzie! My heart skips a beat I'm not quite sure why. I have been feeling bad about how I laughed at him and I could see the hurt in his eyes, and as much as I wanted to avoid him, for my own sake, he has contacted me now. I tell M1 I have to go and hang up the phone.

I don't open the envelope immediately and put it on my bed and just look at it and I am genuinely scared of what he thinks of me and I hate that feeling. I "know" what he must think of me and I don't like the idea that he would think that, yet I know it is justified, which makes me feel even worse. I think about tearing it up, but I know I have to see him on Monday at school, and he would be thinking I know its contents and if he wants me to do something and I don't, will that make things worse?

I open the envelope and inside is a letter. It reads, "Emily I am disappointed in how far we drifted apart since my dad left and we had to move. You were someone I always thought highly of, but it is evident that you don't consider me your friend anymore. I won't go into too much detail about why I have reached that conclusion, but I know I'm right, let's just leave it at that. I want you to know that by the time you read this I would have taken my own life. I don't want to put the blame on you, but I have been consistently bullied by Connors and I know for a fact that you have laughed at this and have witnessed these episodes and chosen to do nothing about it. I know you didn't want others to know that we were friends once, but I didn't expect you to laugh along with them as I got humiliated.

I could have tolerated the fact that you didn't stand up for me, to protect your reputation and keep yourself out of harm's way but seeing you laughing like that was the worst thing that could have happened to me. I realised then that no one really gives a shit about me. I agonised about whether I would send this letter because I think deep down you know what you did was wrong and that if you are anything like the Emily I knew; you would be feeling bad about that as well.

I didn't send this to beat you up, but to ask you to do something for me if you feel anything and want to make things right. I want you to ask yourself, 'What can I do to prevent this happening to someone else?' That's all I want you to do, if I'm wrong about you then no one really does give a shit about me and I won't be around to confirm my suspicion, but it would be great if I was right about you. I picked one song for you which I'm hoping sums up where you are at. I hope you are sorry."

Caught in the Crowd:

(Scan the QR code or hold down Ctrl and click the link)

http://www.youtube.com/watch?v=GIDarYJHCpA

    I quickly look up the song via the link he sent. The song and clip hits me hard. I then have to reread the letter because as bizarre as it sounds, I had to confirm that he said he took his own life. This hits me harder. I can see why he chose the song for me; the guilt is immense. I also apply significant meaning to his call on me having to protect my reputation and keeping myself out of harm's way. I can feel the judgement in that line, I'm not sure if it's real or assumed by me, but I'm crying and I know he is right about me. He can read me like a book, yet I didn't think he was doing it as tough as this. I try not to think about it but keep replaying his face when he saw me laughing that day and now, I know its impact. I start to feel sick. I can't help myself, but I replay the clip he sent a few more times and re-read the letter a few more times. I want to do what he is asking, to make things right, I'm not sure how.

    I suddenly think what if he didn't do it? I decide to call his home and ask for him, pretending I'm someone else, but the phone rings out and I'm not sure. I'm heightened by the fact that there is nothing on Facebook or Twitter, but then Josh isn't all that popular so not likely I would get any clues from that. I don't sleep all night just a nervous feeling and thoughts going through my head makes sure of that.

    Early Sunday morning, I try Josh's house again and this time, a man answers. I ask for Josh and he asks me how I know Josh. I tell him I'm his study partner working on an assignment and I was just checking on whether he was able to find the information for the assignment. There was an uncomfortable silence and I start to fear the worst. The man says that Josh won't be coming back to school and says to wait until Monday as they will notify the school about what is going on. He hangs up and then I know.

    Now I'm in shock, I had been feeling bad before getting his letter then it was disbelief and now just shock. I don't know whether to tell my mum, she used to be friends with his mum a few years ago, but I feel a bit worried to explain how I know. This thought jolts me back to the realisation that the letter and the song choice is specifically telling me I am a contributor that drove him to taking his own life. My head starts to spin and I'm gasping for air. I feel my breakfast coming up and I am running to the toilet, just getting there before I throw up.

    I start to think who else he might have contacted, surely if I got a letter, he would have contacted Steele, so I give him a call. He answers, and I ask him straight out, 'Did you hear from Josh McKenzie?' I can tell from the pause that he has. He says he has, and I tell him about my contact and my phone call to his house and he tells me about the DVD he got and what he saw at Josh's house. We are both convinced now that Josh has definitely gone through with it. We consider the idea that it could be an elaborate hoax and his parents are in on it, but that would appear less likely.

We talk about what if he did actually do it. Steele says he is a bit worried because he is implicated and there are lots of people who witnessed many incidents which involved Josh. He reassures me, probably more than he needs to, that he never meant for this to happen, he says he would have stopped if he had known the effect it was having on Josh. I can detect a crack in his voice and suspect that he is close to tears. He then says he has to go and will see me at school tomorrow and hangs up.

I put on a song Josh and I used to play when we used to hang out a few years ago, it's a touch alternative for me, but it seems appropriate for the situation. The song is a bit haunting and the lyric is a little dark, I sort of want to feel nostalgic and sad at the same time and I cry a little for the Josh I knew back then, and for the Josh I watched get humiliated and I laughed at. They seem like such different people and so far apart in terms of time as well.

Disarm:

(Scan the QR code or hold down Ctrl and click the link)

http://www.youtube.com/watch?v=d1acEVmnVhI

Chapter 7

My name is Ben Gray and I have just got off the phone from Josh Mckenzie's stepfather, Rick, who advised me that Josh had taken his own life. Josh is a student at my school where I have been Principal for the past 11 years. I have had a couple of students pass away in my time, but only one of those had taken their own life before. Death is always a hard thing to deal with, but it is even worse when it is a suicide, because there is often a lot of unanswered questions and what ifs. Josh was a quiet type student, quite unremarkable really, never got in a lot of trouble, couple of scuffles here or there, no real sports activity and middle of the road in his grades. I didn't pay that much attention but he didn't appear to have a large group of friends.

I feel for the family and his friends. It also means I have to plan how we communicate it to his classmates. His stepfather asked that we don't give out details that it was a suicide, but he did indicate that his wife wanted to talk to me, but she was currently busy organising the funeral. I thought the best thing to do was to tell his main class first thing today when their first class was due to start. Then I would talk to Clint Adams about how we can help the kids. Clint is a consultant who has started working with us to help with a Change management system he has developed to help me and my staff work together better as a team. He is then helping us set up specific systems within the classes to help the students treat each other better.

I was present at a public service forum I was invited to by a friend a few months ago and Clint did a presentation on something he called Red Brain / Blue Brain which also included training on the dialogue model, which was from a book I since read called *Crucial Conversations* by the guys at Vital Smarts:

(Scan the QR code or hold down Ctrl and click the link)

http://www.vitalsmarts.com/crucialconversations/

His message made a lot of sense. In a nutshell, he was talking about how we as individuals are wired in our brains and how our natural instincts can actually work against us without us knowing. He also talked about how those natural instincts then affect how we interact and then how that affects relationships that we have with others. It was very interesting so I organised to meet him and take me through an outline of his program. I then talked to him about what we could do to help the kids, to minimise bullying and create a better school environment. He indicated that he usually just worked with adults in a work situation, but he was interested in helping with the students, but needed to work on the content and make some changes. I was able to find some footage of Clint in action at a workplace, the audio is not brilliant and a bit of his PowerPoint presentation did not fit into the screen but you get an idea of what he is talking about.

(Scan the QR code or hold down Ctrl and click the link)

Part 1

https://www.youtube.com/watch?v=tOdlixx_59E&t=26s

Part 2

https://www.youtube.com/watch?v=Xc9wQuZ0A6A

Part 3

https://www.youtube.com/watch?v=0jqo5PRzkkk

Anyway, I will talk to him about how to approach this as he has a very good instinct for people and seems very effective in working with groups. It's almost class time and I rehearse what I'm going to say to the students in my head and start walking over to the class. I have already briefed Miss Bailey about the situation and she meets me at the door. She does look a little shocked, it's tough when this happens and suicide gives another element to the disbelief. As a teacher, Miss Bailey would probably be asking if it's something she did, what could she have done differently? She is a very good teacher, lots of energy loves the students and just a lovely person. You can tell in her eyes that she is not herself, normally she is brimming over with energy but I told her about Josh about an hour ago and it has affected her. She is quite young, early twenties and this would be a very new experience for her and obviously not a pleasant one.

We wait in the class and talk about how she's going and the students start to dawdle in, a little suspicious about my presence. I generally have a good rapport with the students, but me waiting in their class is unusual, so their suspicion is not unexpected. When they are all seated, I stand at the front and address them. I say, 'Guys, I have some bad news, unfortunately on Friday evening one of your classmates, Joshua McKenzie passed away. His funeral is this Thursday afternoon at 3 pm at the funeral parlour on Coppards Road in Newcomb. As we get more details, we will let you know. We have cancelled your class after lunch, so you have some time to soak in the information, talk to each other and we can discuss it then to see what your thoughts are.'

One of the students, Meg Reynolds, looks upset but asks how it happened. I tell her we don't know all the details other than he passed away Friday evening. I can tell they aren't "buying" it but I wanted to honour the wishes of his family. I leave the class, but not before I advise Miss Bailey that if she wishes she can scrap today's lessons and do something a bit less taxing on the students.

I ring Clint Adams, who is a ball of enthusiasm, and even answering his phone you can sense he has a smile on his face. I tell him about Josh and enquire as to how we should tackle it. He says he will come over right away and discuss the options with me.

He arrives an hour later and he goes through some options to consider when talking to the kids. I tell him I got a call from the police and they want to interview some of the students. He says we should get the students in the lecture theatre after lunch and talk about Josh and what their thoughts are.

I organise the session in the lecture theatre and although I get there early, Clint is in there already interacting with students. He is definitely a people person and is never uncomfortable talking to anyone and there he is talking to one of the students, Taylor Harper. She is a little alternative, very shy and an OK student. I think she was probably one of Josh's friends, but I'm not sure.

Chapter 8

My name is Taylor Harper and I just found out that one of my classmates Josh McKenzie has died and my head is swimming. I had always liked him, from afar, never really had the courage to tell him. I secretly hoped he liked me and would ask me out. I got close to being friends with him a few months ago, by hanging out with him and his two friends. We would hang out at lunch time and talk about stuff. He was into '80s' things, music, clothes and video games. He was right into the retro, classic stuff, but he loved older sports champions. He would talk about Michael Jordan and Muhammed Ali and guys like that. I like his sense of humour; it was a little dark and sarcastic and I liked that about him. He always had an underlying sadness, I never really knew why, but I suspected it had something to do with his dad, who left him and his Mum. I don't know the full story, he never really shared that, but there was enough to know it had an effect on him.

I really liked him and thought he was cute. He was also so shy, like I was and I came close on many occasions to asking him out, but would chicken out, because I couldn't stand the humiliation if he laughed at me and I just couldn't handle that kind of rejection, so I never did. The funny thing is I would look for "signs" of what he would do if I asked him. I would listen for songs or read horoscopes looking for confirmation anywhere to build up courage to ask him. I just could never overcome the fear that he might say no and then I would go home and be so angry with myself. On the one hand I would just want to know once and for all, but on the other hand I didn't want to know if he didn't feel the same way, so I would do nothing.

The news that he was dead hits me like a tonne of bricks. After our principal tells us, we all just sit there and I look over at Steele, who has been Josh's tormentor. He is just sitting there looking into space. I was half expecting him to be smiling and it surprises me that he even looks a bit sad. He definitely is not his usual cocky self. I have seen him do a lot of nasty things to Josh, and I also think that a change in Josh came a while ago after an incident with Steele, which humiliated him in front of a lot of people. Josh seemed to withdraw from his two friends and me and they never really tried to support him too much. I know we talked afterwards and justified why we didn't stand up for him, but I don't think we convinced ourselves, so we didn't really talk about it anymore. It's difficult to accept that you are gutless, so it's better to ignore that fact. I cry in class, for Josh, for missed opportunities and for not having the courage to at least stand up for him. My self-preservation took precedence. I was someone who passed unnoticed to those who determine whether I would get grief or not. Unfortunately Josh was not so lucky and I would be lying if I said this didn't cross my mind when hanging out with Josh.

No one likes to draw "bad" attention to themselves, so when you are under the radar, then hanging out with others who are on the radar puts you at risk. I suspect he has killed himself as they give no details of what happened, which if it was an accident or something like that they could easily say, but their silence on the issue is suspicious. I question my courage and I also question how my own reaction and that of his friends contributed to him killing himself, I want to say "taking his own life", because somehow it sounds a bit better than "killing himself", but it is just that. The whole class is so quiet, I'm surprised to see "glamour girl" Emily Ross looking like she had a tear in her eye. This is very surprising because she always seems so up herself and never really even spoke to Josh, so I'm not sure what that's about.

I look around the room and it is quite sombre, even though he never had a large circle of friends I guess at a basic level of humanity no one really wanted him dead. This thought of "circle of friends" reminds me of a song, I check it out on my iPhone, the teacher is in shock so doesn't really care about teaching us today so I check it out.

Edie Brickell & the New Bohemian's *Circle*:

(Scan the QR code or hold down Ctrl and click the link)

http://www.youtube.com/watch?v=q_GkjymuQ9U

The song takes on a new meaning. Listening to the lyrics, definitely describes where Josh was at, he did disengage from us. The lyrics seems to resonate with me that he might have been feeling like being alone was the best thing for him so we couldn't hurt him by abandoning him, he would do it himself. It was better to deal with things alone, because it was somehow easier to deal with, given his public humiliation and our lack of support. This thought just makes me feel awful, that we couldn't support him and I was so gutless that I did nothing and he had to fight his secret war in his own head and lost. This prompts another song I remember had that exact line in it. It's an old '80s' song Josh would actually play. I play that too.

Concrete Blonde's *Joey*:

(Scan the QR code or hold down Ctrl and click the link)

http://www.youtube.com/watch?v=OdpTcvSn8HQ

The line wasn't quite there but I'm surprised by the things that spring to mind. The whole day after that is just a jumble of thoughts, questions and disbelief.

I'm not an angry person and I never really had any kind of fight, or ever stand up for myself and I don't know what comes over me but I feel anger building up inside me. I'm angry with myself for not doing more, I'm angry with Josh's friends for also being so piss weak and I'm even more angry with that prick, Steele for taking it upon himself to humiliate Josh to the point that he may have done this. The anger overwhelms me and as much as I weigh up the possible outcomes of what I'm about to do, I'm up on my feet almost without really thinking and approach Steele, he looks up at me and I feel the tears welling up and they break free from my eyes and heat my cheeks as they roll down.

I'm not sure exactly what I scream at him, but it's not pleasant, I let him have it. I then surprise myself even further and I physically attack him, the first three or so punches hit their mark, right on his nose.

Time seems to slow as I hit him, I'm not sure if he is surprised by my attack, but he seems slow to react and doesn't seem to be defending himself, so he copes a few more blows, until I feel someone holding me back. He's on the ground now and I'm almost sitting on his chest and still punching. I see blood flowing freely from his nose and I want to see more. I try to punch, but I'm being dragged off him, I'm suddenly exhausted and am actually glad I'm being dragged off, I'm suddenly "back" in class, I start to notice sounds and people again. It's a weird sensation, but I then realise I'm being held by my teacher and two other boys in my class. I don't resist anymore and I let them sit me down. Steele lays on the ground and doesn't get up immediately. I'm surprised when he finally does and instead of an angry response he looks like a man defeated. I see real pain in his face and I'm sure it's not from my punches. The realisation that he has been confronted with what he did to Josh and what Josh then did to himself is written all over his face and in that instant, I feel sorry for him. He has blood on his hands and he doesn't know what to do. I want to say, 'Serves you right, I hope he haunts you!' But I don't. Although, I genuinely feel pity for him.

As I'm being dragged away, I think of a song where a person loses someone close to them and their memory is so painful, they actually feel "haunted" by that person and yet it's only that person's own thoughts and memories that is haunting them. The idea shoots through my head and I know Steele is feeling that right now, or at least I hope he is. I get taken to our sick bay and I fall asleep with the song in my head, I'm so tired.

Evanescence, *My Immortal*:

(Scan the QR code or hold down Ctrl and click the link)

http://www.youtube.com/watch?v=5anLPw0Efmo

Chapter 9

I can't believe when the principal tells us Josh is dead, which confirms that it isn't some elaborate joke. I look at Emily but her head is down, I sit there and reality bites, and it BITES hard. Although I already knew this, I realise I was hoping that it actually wasn't true that Josh would turn up and laugh at me and it was a joke. But it's not and he is dead and I realise that him sending me the DVD was real and I am responsible for his death, and he made a point of telling me that. I sit there blankly looking ahead. I start to think of what this could mean for me. Can I be held responsible for his death? I am really scared now because I'm not sure who else he sent DVDs to, he also threatened me in the DVD about having sent information to another person, and I start to think who he may have chosen?

The next thing I know one of the girls in my class, Taylor Harper, gets up and walks over to me. She is one of those people in my class I never really took any notice of, you could say she flies under the radar, doesn't draw much attention to herself. She is not unattractive; she is very quiet and as she is standing in front of me, I realise she is kind of cute and that I guess I never really noticed her before.

Suddenly, she is yelling abuse at me and then she's punching me. Part of my reaction was shock, but part was also the fact that I suddenly thought she was cute and there was also an element of guilt, because what she was yelling was clearly blaming me for Josh's death. I did not really defend myself and copped what she gave, until she was dragged off me. I wanted to be punished, I felt an empty feeling inside. It's hard to describe when you start to ask questions of yourself and the answers are not good. After they drag her off me and out of the class, I sit there just thinking. I start asking myself why I actually did those things to Josh, and I honestly can't answer that. I assume I was getting some enjoyment out of it, but right now I can't recall that. I have this pit in my stomach and start to feel quite ill.

I'm scared to look around the classroom, I feel lots of eyes on me and I'm not sure if that feeling is real or imagined, because I don't want to know so I just put my head on my arms and face the desk and start to cry. I want to stop, but I lose that battle. I lay there for a while and my mind is filled with many instances of me doing things to Josh. Suddenly, they don't seem so funny and I start to realise just how many instances there have been. I'm genuinely shocked because I hadn't really given the impact it might have had much thought. It's a scary thought when you realise that you had a massive impact on someone else taking their life. I never thought much of Josh in the past, I know I didn't want him dead and while he had fought back a few times, I was always too strong for him. I try to think of any signs that he was struggling with me picking on him, because I have been doing things to him for a while now and he never seemed to take one any worse than the other. I don't know what to think anymore. I drift in and out of sleep, we do no school work and Taylor's crack at me makes the mood in class even more uncomfortable. For the first time I feel like I'm on the outside, I'm not myself and no one wants to be associated with me. Again I'm not sure if that is real or imagined and again, I don't look around, fearful I might be right.

I kill time checking out YouTube on my iPhone and type in what I'm really feeling. I want to be taken away and stumble across two songs with that title.

The first by Lifehouse is a slower song which feeds my mood, it's slower and reinforces how I'm feeling. How cool is the guitarist he bobs his head in a cool way.

Lifehouse – *Take Me Away.*

(Scan the QR code or hold down Ctrl and click the link)

https://www.youtube.com/watch?v=NX4x4YkY3Os

The second song surprises me, it's unusually cool and surprisingly upbeat. It lifts my spirits a little and I play it a few times. I challenge you to try singing the first bit without doing a chipmunk voice!

Fortune Family's – *Take Me Away.*

(Scan the QR code or hold down Ctrl and click the link)

http://www.youtube.com/watch?v=9V_F8vqKb5o

I'm woken by the other students starting to exit the classroom and when I look up, I see they are following our teacher, principal and some other dark-skinned guy I have seen at the school before, but I'm not sure if he is a teacher or not. I tag along and we all end up in our lecture theatre and our principal addresses us. I notice Taylor has met the group here, she doesn't look at me and I can see from the redness, of her eyes that she had been crying. The mood is sombre and I half listen to the principal telling us that if any of us want some help to deal with Josh's death that we can speak to the chaplain. He then introduces the other guy as Clint Adams, someone the school has been working with who is some change management guru who is helping them do some things to change their work environment and the intent was he would then help them do some of that work with the students, but with what's happened with Josh he is going to start with our class in the next few weeks. I drift in and out of what he is saying, I have this horrible feeling in my stomach and I guess it's a real fear of what could happen to me.

The rest of the day is a bit of a blur for me. I don't have any further episodes with anyone else, but there is a definite coldness from the others towards me. I saw little groups of them talking among themselves and looking at me. I know they were saying things about me. Not one of them actually came up to talk to me. I saw the two Emily's briefly but they were surrounded by others, and I really didn't feel like talking to anyone. I go home and I still can't shrug the feeling of anxiety since I officially found out that Josh was dead. I suddenly think of the old couple who came out of his house on the weekend and I get a surge of adrenaline I guess, and I suddenly feel sick and I vomit on the lawn of some random house. The thought that this was probably his grandparents and they had just lost their grandson makes me very queasy. I suddenly think about my grandparents, who I am quite close to and what they would do if it was me who had died. The feeling to vomit again hits me and I dry retch a few times, but nothing comes out, I'm suddenly running and crying.

I get home and my sister, Grace, is home. She looks at me and with the observation skills of a hawk tells me I look like shit. She also tells me she heard about Josh, our principal apparently went class to class and notified them all that a student had died. She knows the issues Josh had with me and I'm surprised when she asks me if I'm OK. I don't know what overcomes me but I break down into tears and keep saying, '*I didn't want him to die.*' She hugs me for a while and says soothing words, I'm not sure exactly but I know she is trying.

After I calm down a bit, we have a lengthy conversation about things. I tell her about the DVD and then show her. I tell her about me going to his house on the weekend and what I saw. I also tell her about Emily's DVD and what happened today with Taylor. I can tell from her expression that this could be serious for me. She's usually very calm and jokes with me, but there is not even a hint of that. It worries me more because she is usually so calm. She says something that scares me even more, '*You have to tell Dad, he'll know what to do!*' My head starts to swim and I have to run to the toilet, the stress and feeling of being out of control just overwhelms me. I don't make it to the toilet, the next thing I'm doing is cleaning up a mess on the tiles.

I feel so drained and I go to my room and go straight to sleep. The next thing I know both my parents are in my room with concerned faces. Grace has obviously told them and they throw lots of questions at me. I was initially scared to tell them and was very anxious about that, but now that they know, I feel a bit better as I explain everything to them. It's not a nice thing to tell your parents that you are responsible for someone taking their own life. There are no ifs, buts or maybe's either. He sent me a DVD and a letter to confirm his view on my part. No point sugar-coating it to save myself, it is what it is, and the realisation is awful to deal with, so I tell them the lot. They ask to watch the DVD which I show to them. When it's over, they sit silent for a while.

Dad then starts to formulate a plan. He notes that in the DVD, Josh doesn't say he wants to dob me in, he is giving me a second chance, which he assumes means Josh hasn't told anyone just yet which means that if I cop any "heat" it has no support from Josh, unless of course he lied in the DVD, but we don't suspect he has. For the first time in a long time, I'm actually impressed by my dad. It's like his energy level jumped up, he's motivated and is almost like a lawyer who is thinking of some kind of strategy to keep me out of jail. I have never seen him like this. My mum also surprised me as she went into "protective" mode throwing ideas in terms of how they can keep me out of harm's way. For the first time in a long time all of the Connors are in one room and working together. The scary thing is it takes someone to die for this to happen, and I feel another injection of pain as I think of Josh lying dead somewhere and his family grieving probably hating me, I'm not even sure. I feel some solace in the fact that is has shown me my family gives a shit.

That night I start looking up songs and articles about bullying and suicide and find a really old song based on a girl who goes and shoots kids in a school, it's kind of appropriate because I'm not liking this Monday right now.

Boomtown Rats: *Don't like Mondays*:

(Scan the QR code or hold down Ctrl and click the link)

http://www.youtube.com/watch?v=-Kobdb37Cwc

Info on song:

http://en.wikipedia.org/wiki/I_Don't_Like_Mondays

The lyrics prompt me to think of what Josh would have thought of school. He would have hated Mondays, facing me, knowing I would be doing something to humiliate him or hurt him. It's hard to hide from yourself. So I need to face up to me and change that "old" me.

Chapter 10

The day is here and I'm in a storm, I'm "floating" I can't describe it any other way. Rick is awesome, he has everything organised, I have been strong because of what Josh asked me to do, but I can't lie to myself, I'm struggling and I'm so scared I will crack today. I can't bear to think about Josh's coffin coming out and having to sit there for an hour or so while we play his songs and show photos, which I had to pick for his "clip" it's an awful experience. I stopped crying though, I have been listening to the songs he chose and the song *Titanium* resonates with me, it's an empowering song and it gives me some strength. I hum the tune in my head as we leave the house to go to the school chapel. I feel OK.

We are one of the first to arrive, I'm just a little numb and although I'm there I'm almost unaware of things, it's a strange feeling but even though I know things and people are there it's like I'm not capable of totally acknowledging them. People come up and offer their condolences but I don't even hear what they are saying, I pretend I do and say something like thank you, but I'm not even sure.

The whole thing goes quicker than I thought and the numbness makes it quite unemotional for me. I surprise myself that I don't really cry until his clip goes up and *These Days* starts to play.

(Scan the QR code or hold down Ctrl and click the link)

https://www.youtube.com/watch?v=DpWVsOyf0n4

The old photos of him as a little boy, his first days of school, his first football game, photos of us on the beach when he was still a happy boy. The grief hits me like a freight train, I actually didn't see it coming and I pass out.

I come to and I'm lying on the bench still in the chapel, Rick is holding me up and suddenly I'm back. I haven't been out too long because the song is still playing. I tell Rick for them to just keep going, so the service continues without any incident from me. I sit through the service, I'm not religious and never have been, I'm not sure this is what Josh wanted, he didn't say and I get an unreal feeling this is not what he would have wanted. I just don't want to be here. I grit my teeth and plough through. I have a greater appreciation of parents when you see them on TV when something bad happened and their child dies earlier than expected. It's a horrendous feeling no one can explain or comprehend until it happens to them.

The fact that it was self-inflicted narrows the participants even further, because you find yourself blaming the same person you are there to mourn, but you also ask questions of yourself as a parent and the end result tells you that you failed. You can't be OK and have this outcome. You have to be below that, you didn't pass! I didn't pass, I was a dismal failure, not once but twice. I compose my instinct to throw up, but my mind asks questions of me and I can't justify how weak I have been for Josh. I question why I wasn't more involved. He did tell me things about school and I let Rick tell him to toughen up, this wasn't once, we kept telling him the same thing. I agreed he needed to toughen up and I agreed he was too timid. The sad thing is I know we didn't give him any tools or do anything to help him not be timid and change what was happening to him. I start to feel sorry for myself and I know I could curl up into a ball and just hide again, but his letter was so explicit that I not do that and this keeps me out of there. I find a strength he knew was there and I grit my teeth. **I'm Back!**

I don't cry again that day. They take Josh away and I know I have moved past his death. I had the same experience when my first husband left us. I struggled a lot longer, but then all of a sudden, I was out the other end. I guess your mind has to come to grips with whatever is going on before you can move on. Josh forced me to get there quicker. I have a steely resolve to do this right as he asked me to. I have nothing else to help him so I "have" to do this, to fail him again would be unbearable. We all go to the reception centre and I'm surprised by how many people there are. I'm not sure if they were at the service, I guess I never really looked to see. The school students dominate as I see their uniforms and it takes me to his first day of high school, him with this huge back-pack on his back, his floppy sun hat with the school logo, proud as punch that he was a BIG kid now. I choke up again but I don't cry, it's a close second option, but I choose the path Josh asked. I am happy to see so many students, the Principal is a nice man and he stands there with a few of Josh's teachers.

I play the dutiful hostess serving food and drinks with a smile I manufacture and act my way through, everyone is so polite and offer condolences. I guess we all do that. I have always been at the other end and as much as it's a nice gesture, I realise it does nothing to help. Then something happens that staggers me.

A man I don't know, dark-skinned, but not black, with what I can only say is an inviting face comes up to me, his green eyes have a happy essence to them, he seems like a nice person. He introduces himself as Clint Adams, the name rings no bells, he says he needs to talk to me privately, but not today. The bit that staggers me is he says Josh sent him a letter, but needs to talk to me when the funeral is done, not with Rick or anyone else. He kisses my hands and tells me he will call me in a couple of days and before I can respond he is gone.

I don't know how to respond; I ask why would Josh send a letter to a complete stranger? I question whether he was a stranger to Josh and whether there are other letters I'm not aware of? I ask myself a lot of questions when everyone has left, I sit and look at old photos and replay the DVD we made with photos and the songs he chose, it makes me think of an old John Lennon song.

Beautiful Boy:

(Scan the QR code or hold down Ctrl and click the link)

http://www.youtube.com/watch?v=Lt3IOdDE5iA

I cry myself to sleep.

Chapter 11

It's been two days and I'm anxious to find out who this Clint Adams is and why Josh would send him a letter. I had Googled him and he appears to be a Change Management consultant who has worked in heavy industry and schools. I contacted the principal to see if he was a teacher at the school and he advises that Clint was employed to do some work with the teachers to help them as a group to do better and improve their own group dynamics. I organised to meet with Clint the next day.

On the morning I agree for him to meet me at home and he turns up 5 minutes early and I let him in. After some basic chit-chat I can tell that he knows I'm anxious to hear why he got a letter from Josh and also the contents of that letter. He then proceeds to tell me that he had never officially met Josh, but he received a letter in the mail to his business address. He hands me the letter and it reads,

My name is Josh McKenzie, a student at Ben Gray's school, if you are reading this, I will already be dead. I am writing to you because I know you are working with the school to help the teachers work better together. I checked you out and found some information and feel confident you can do what I need to help others like me and also help others who bully others like me. I know it's not a clear-cut problem, but I'm in such a shit headspace right now I can't see or wait for a solution to help me. I just have no desire to live, the pain of living is just horrible, I look in the mirror and I can't face myself.

Enough about me though. I have sent DVDs to fellow students, people I guess had an impact on where my head is at right now. I don't wish them harm, but I need something good to come out of my death.

I chose you because I heard you are a decent man who is very good at what you do and for some reason, I know you can help me and I go to my grave knowing this to be the case. I need you to work with Steele Connors who is a bully, but I want you to help him change his ways, I also want you to work with the two Emilys in my class, as they rule the roost and don't realise how they bring on some of his behaviour. I would also like you to work with all our students to help prevent this happening to others. I don't know how you do that but I read your profile and checked you out on YouTube and I have a good feeling about you.

Last but not least I want you to contact my mum because she does not cope with this type of thing, so I need you to help her be strong and also stop her from wanting to do anything to Steele as a plot of vengeance. This is about doing better not punishment. I don't want punishment; I want things to be better. Please Mr Adams all I want is for this not to happen to anyone else, but also please look after my mum she might need it. I did tell Steele in the message I sent him that I also sent information to certain people and they would go to the police if he didn't change his ways. I don't want punishment, but if he doesn't want to be part of a solution then consider what else can be done. I trust your judgement on this. Thank you, Clint.

Sincerely Yours,
Josh.

I sit and look blankly at the letter not sure what to say. After a brief silence Clint says he can do what Josh has asked him to do, but he needs me to firstly deal with the Steele component of it. I had very little idea of who exactly was having this effect on him until now. I remember a couple of fights that I was called into school about and I am sure it was this Steele Connors boy involved, but Josh never really made out that was a big deal. He was quiet and withdrew from us a little, but I thought that was normal teenage boy behaviour, plus Rick and I got married and had Georgia which we assumed also took some of our attention from him. Thinking back now it was easy to think he needed space, and maybe he was too "proud" I'm not sure if that's the right word, maybe too "scared" to say it to me. Was it me or was it Rick, did he not want to say anything because of Rick? I guess a young man might feel a little embarrassed to say to his stepdad that he is being bullied. In an instant, things flood into my head and it's not good. I remember a fight Josh had with Rick, where he said to, "suck it up" or something like that and something about it being character building. Josh was angry and stormed off and went to his room. I wasn't fully aware of what happened, but maybe Josh went to Rick to help him and he told him to suck it up and grow from it.

This thought is horrible to me, how do I deal with that if it is true? I can't think about that now. I have to focus on what we can do going forward.

I ask Clint what exactly he wants me to do to deal with the Steele Connors issue. I know he means the blame I would place on him and the pain that it has now led me to. In my head it's funny, because Josh anticipated my thoughts and I have already "convinced" myself of what could come. I have to be honest with myself, I can't hide from myself, and I always "knew" Josh was being bullied but did nothing about it. I guess I hoped it would go away, that he would deal with it and the issue would disappear. Clint and I talk for a while and he has this annoying thing he does where he keeps throwing questions at me, questions I know I wouldn't want to ask myself, because I have been hiding from the answers. He questions me and I find myself short of the mark. Damn it's awful when you "know", it's time to face up to you, no more trying to convince yourself that your actions are justified.

I acknowledge that I knew Josh was struggling, that I sided with Rick's view that Josh needed to grow up and suck it up, even though I knew that was not right. I want to blame Rick and this Steele kid, but Clint keeps asking me questions and I'm in a really honest state for the first time in my life and I keep pointing to myself. I know others have contributed, but I could have done things too. I look at this guy who I only just met and his questions leave me so "naked" so vulnerable. I know his intent is to help me, there is something about him which is so engaging, so calming, it's like I trust him implicitly. I'm not sure if it's because Josh chose to involve him or if he is that good, but he seems to know his stuff and his questions open more for me and actually as painful as it is, it seems to help me.

After he stops questioning me I come to the cold hard blatant fact that I already knew what was happening with Josh, but was too "scared" to challenge Rick's thoughts on what should happen, I was too gutless to challenge the school and insist on better intervention, but I also understand with my discussion with Clint that they also wanted the problem to go away and didn't really know how to deal with it. As much as this discussion is very confronting for me and very emotional (I cried a lot and it might appear that it went quick it was a few hours), it was also cleansing. I didn't realise how much I already knew and actually didn't deal with, which meant I always felt bad about it. Clint was great because he got it all out of me and just when I felt as bad as I could, he said, 'So what can YOU do to make this better?'

It was such a great question, because I had been feeling so bad and confronting myself and being brutally honest, I wasn't feeling all that happy with myself, so the question seemed to change my focus. I find it funny because I know I'm being "played" and while I would normally push against this, I was also relieved in some weird way that I was exposing these things to myself. It was a little liberating, but confronting at the same time. It's hard to feel good about the realisation that you were a significant contributing factor to your son's suicide. I cried quite a lot, but his question, 'So what can YOU do to make this better?' snaps me back and I'm asking myself this question. What can I do? I ponder the thought and lots of different things come to mind, Clint and I discuss them and he leaves after I thank him.

I'm suddenly energised, my focus is on a "future" state as Clint called it. He talked about this term he calls "Red Brain" which as he explains it, is our natural instinctive reactions to "Fight or Flight", which can become a problem if we stay in that state too long or too often. He explains it a lot better than I, but he said if we change focus to a future state, it forces us to use a different part of the brain, which then changes the brain activity and changing the brain chemistry in the process. It clearly works because I haven't felt this good since Josh died. My mind is awash with ideas of what I can do to make things better. I put on a Guy Sebastien's song which is cool and also quite meaningful.

Guy Sebastien: *Battle Scars*:

(Scan the QR code or hold down Ctrl and click the link)

http://www.youtube.com/watch?v=4ka1Lgd3SAI

I actually sleep very well and I am feeling better about things. I wake up with a spring in my step, some kind of purpose, I'm not sure yet but my mood is up and I feel good for the first time in what seems like ages.

I call Clint and we have a brief discussion on the phone and I want to focus on what I do about the Steele issue. To his credit and my annoyance, he asks me, 'What do you think you should do, especially given Josh emphasised he does not want punishment?'

I sit and ponder, and believe me I had thought about this, because Clint gave me the letter and I am very aware of what Josh wants. The implication of me as weak is also in the letter and I "know" he is right, I have never been the strong one, I have relied on others to get me through, even Josh, which scares me given what he just did. I find what I can only call my "steely resolve", my new attitude, I'm going to do something about this and do it well! I let my little boy down and that just can't happen in this case!

I say, 'I want to meet him and his parents.' They all need to know that we know he was a factor in Josh's death, and they also need to know Josh's wishes to get Steele to turn his behaviour around and make things better for others like him.

Clint agrees with this but takes me through something called the dialogue model.

(Scan the QR code or hold down Ctrl and click the link)

http://agilecoffee.com/toolkit/crucial-conversations/

He tells me that knowing how a conversation occurs, but also being mindful of the story I tell myself and the "feeling" part of the model is crucial and is related to the red brain stuff he took me through earlier. He says it is important to stay in Blue Brain so that I don't become aggressive or defensive and actually say what I need to say.

The fact that he is talking me through this stuff makes me realise that like Josh, he "knows" that I need help to not go to pieces when confronted with these people. I know that I avoid confrontation and I am that person who secretly seethes when someone pushes in line, but I won't say a damn thing, I am aware why that is now. My fear stops me. I think about that and wonder why? I suppose the fear is that someone won't like me even though they pushed in, I still feel uncomfortable saying, 'Excuse me, sir, the line is actually behind me.' This Blue Brain stuff is very real, I think of events and how I dealt with it and I know now I went into Red Brain. I constantly replayed the same things in my head, "the story I told myself" and it took me to Red Brain and I never got out of it until I told myself a different story. It makes so much more sense now.

I wish Clint had told me this stuff a long time ago. His video on YouTube is even more insightful as he talked about experience and mental models and when I think about it.

Blue Brain/Red Brain.

(Scan the QR code or hold down Ctrl and click the link)

http://www.youtube.com/watch?v=tOdlixx_59E

I know that because my dad was verbally abusive to my mum and she and all the kids were in fear, we tended not to speak up, because he would be so aggressive, so we avoided that situation and our mental models were formed. I look back now and I am defensive and I want people to like me, I wanted my dad to like me! He was having an affair and actually said to me he didn't want me and my sisters, he wanted to leave us and live with this other woman. Back then my mum didn't want him to go and I would hear them fighting for a while, but he left and things seemed to get better. But my mother was this bitter person for a while, she never got depressive, but she would constantly talk about what he did to her for years until she finally met her current partner.

I remember before she met him, we would want to avoid her because she was like this broken record, we tried to talk to her about moving on, but somehow all her conversations would lead back to Dad and what he did to her and we would hear this recurring story again and again. It still makes me sad that my dad left us like that and then I had to live through the same scenario for me and Josh.

I think about how I would have done things differently had I known this stuff and know I will be a very different person from now on. I can feel a bit more strength and surety in myself now. The sad thing is that Josh organised me to meet Clint and in a short space of time it has changed my thinking, I wish he had done the same for himself, Clint might have helped him look at his situation differently and done something about it. This thought makes me feel angry and sad at the same time and I "catch" myself doing this which is taking me to Red Brain again, so I do what Clint suggested, which is to ask myself a high-level question to take me back into Blue Brain. Just asking myself what question I should ask myself does seem to do what he says, it makes me shift gears in my head. I feel myself calming and not as angry as before. I advise myself that this thinking is not good for me, I am quite deliberate about what conversation I have in my head and for the first time in my life I actually think I have control of my thoughts, whereas in the past I suppose I would let events drive me to a defensive Red Brain space, but in the past I tended to stay there for prolonged periods and it only really seemed to shift with significant time.

Chapter 12

Attending Josh's funeral was difficult. Since I lost it in class with Steele and bopped him on his nose, he seems to have avoided me. The days after that, leading up to the funeral, Steele was a little sheepish, he almost looked depressed and rightfully so. I notice that even his usual crew have distanced themselves a bit from him. There is definitely a "numbness" across the school. At night I have been going home and deliberately listening to songs that have a focus on death and other dark connotations. I particularly like these two, Muse: *Madness:*

(Scan the QR code or hold down Ctrl and click the link)

http://www.youtube.com/watch?v=Ek0SgwWmF9w

The offspring: *Gone Away*:

http://www.youtube.com/watch?v=2d3AqlKfXbE

While listening I actually think about how people do go mad and how what they think about can have such an impact on what they do. I especially wonder what Josh was thinking when he took his own life. It has been unofficially confirmed it was suicide, as word has got out that Josh sent out letters and DVD's to Emily and possibly Steele. A shot of pain shoots through me and wish I could have supported him, he probably died thinking no one cared and that there was no way out for him. It pains me that he didn't know how I felt about him; I find myself crying quite a bit. It is a combination of feeling sad that he died alone, thinking he was alone and I'm sure he felt some shame for the humiliation Steele bestowed upon him. Couple that with my regret that I never told him how I felt and also, I never got to find out if he even thought anything like that about me and now, I will never know.

The days leading up to the funeral is a bit of a haze and on the day, I sit through the service without taking that much in. It's sad to see his mum who I hear is who actually found him when he hung himself and then watch the whole thing overwhelm her as she passes out briefly before ploughing on to get through the rest of the service. The songs he chose are sad, especially when they are accompanied by photos of him growing up. The whole class got to come, but I notice that Steele is a noticeable "no show". I can't blame him really, I actually give him some credit, and even he has some conscience.

I'm a little surprised to see Emily Ross crying, she never said two words to Josh, but apparently did get a letter. I guess any time a young person dies there is an element of sadness. In this case it is even sadder given that it could have been preventable. Thinking about this flips my stomach and I actually start to feel nauseous. I feel guilty that I knew he was struggling after the chocolate milk incident, but I thought he wouldn't want me consoling him, that me actually doing that would add an even bigger element of shame for him. I chose to deliberately stay away from him until he was ready to talk again, but I guess it sent him the message that I didn't want to be associated with him and this meant he withdrew from me even more. Again, I have this feeling of guilt for not doing more to help him and support him and regret, for not telling him how I felt about him. My mind starts to wander after a while and I think of the last time I saw Josh laughing and joking with me and I actually smile and cry at the same time. I think of a song he would sing and put on an Irish accent as he sang it by Mumford & Sons:

Little Lion Man:

(Scan the QR code or hold down Ctrl and click the link)

https://www.youtube.com/watch?v=lLJf9qJHR3E

I don't remember the rest of the funeral I just remember being ushered out and back to class. Our principal addresses all of us and mentions something about Clint Adams doing some work with us in a few days' time.

I go home feeling a bit drained and flop on my bed and just start to think about Josh, I try not to beat myself up, but the same thought goes through my head that I could have done so much more and that I just don't know if I can bear the regret of not telling him how I felt. I thought about it so many times in the confines of this room and as much as I wanted him to know I got so scared that he would not feel the same way. I couldn't stand the thought of me being rejected by him, so in some bizarre way I preferred to not know and the idea that he might like me was enough, but at the same time it wasn't I wanted more and I was too gutless. Now I sit here in the cold hard realisation that I will never know. I really don't know what to do, I wish my parents and I had any real relationship, they wouldn't even know how upset I am or that I even liked Josh and that he died. I suddenly feel more alone than ever. I think back to Josh and one time I was with him and a couple of other friends and he was playing some mixed CD of music he made, it contained all this '80s' music which was what he enjoyed. I just remember one song which now springs to mind, which seems appropriate even though it might be a little too late. I play it and drift off to sleep.

    Stevie Nicks: *Talk to Me.*

(Scan the QR code or hold down Ctrl and click the link)

https://www.youtube.com/watch?v=UQl62w71Ets

Chapter 13

I wasn't sure I wanted to go to Josh's funeral. I found myself, after getting the message from Josh and then having his death confirmed at school, that I couldn't really look at Steele the same way. I saw how Taylor reacted in class by just smashing him in the face and I heard what others were saying about Steele, and blaming him for what happened. Even M1 was talking to me about how we should avoid him unless we want to commit social suicide. I was a little shocked how quickly Steele was considered a "leper" by the group. I found myself in two minds about whether to go over and talk to him and support him, but at the same time I felt a lot of pressure from everyone to do the opposite. While I had the dilemma in my head I chose to go with the group and I never really spoke to him about it before the funeral. Steele seemed quite depressed and looked extremely shocked by what happened, the fight and also how we treated him. I felt bad, but the fear of having the same thing happen to me was real, given how quickly they jumped off someone as popular as Steele. I wasn't prepared to put myself in the position where I could be ostracised by others, I wasn't sure I could handle it, so I followed M1's lead.

I think a fair bit about Josh and while I knew Steele was doing things to him that wasn't very good, I never really knew it was taking such a heavy toll on him. I start to think about how I might have felt if those things happened to me and I begin to realise how it would have felt to him, people laughing and not just anyone, but people like me, who he might have considered a friend once. I guess that's why he chose that song for me in my DVD. I wish I knew he was feeling this way, but then I catch myself and ask, *Would I have done anything to help him?* I have to be honest, I'm not really sure. I don't think of myself as a courageous person. If anything, I start to think about this a bit more and I recognise that I do a lot of things and also I don't do a lot of things, because I'm so worried what others will think and it's not necessarily what I would do if no one was there to judge me. I am still shocked that Josh was feeling this bad about events and I think of a Pink song which seems appropriate:

Who Knew:

(Scan the QR code or hold down Ctrl and click the link)

http://www.youtube.com/watch?v=NJWIbIe0N90

I go to Josh's funeral and I'm surprised how emotional I am. I sit and cry throughout the service, as much as I don't really want others to see it. I can't help myself and eventually give up trying to hide it. I know I can make up a story on how sad his mum was and that no young person should die before their parents. Josh's mum faints at one point, which adds weight to my argument, but also makes me even sadder. I see Taylor Harper watching me intently. I knew that she used to hang out with Josh, but clearly from her little boot camp boxing campaign on Steele's face, she may have been more than that. She doesn't make me uneasy and I think she's a little shocked by my reaction as I'm sure many others are. I do notice that Steele is a noticeable absentee. I guess he knew it would have been in bad taste and may have upset a few more people, including him, I really don't think he is in a good headspace.

I focus on the service which is extremely sad especially watching Josh's photos scroll through to the music he chose.

After the service, we go back to class where Mr Gray addresses us and tells us that Clint Adams, the consultant who spoke to us when Josh first died, will be running some sessions with us. I'm not sure what that involves, but I suspect some type of counselling to help us deal with his death. I go home and just think about how fragile life is. I think of my dad so far away and even though Mum and I are in the same house, we don't really talk much. I pretty much come home, have dinner and go to my room until the next day. On weekends we don't really do much, I know Mum misses Dad too and I guess I'm not helping the situation. It suddenly hits me that Mum knows Josh and his mum and I'm not sure anyone told her he had died.

I tell Mum what had happened and she shows no real reaction at first and then for the first time in a long time she comes and gives me a big hug. I realise I had been crying and she could see how upset I was. I hug her back and let the emotion flow. I finally tell her about the DVD I received from Josh, which shocks her. She asks me how I feel about that and we talk through the guilt I feel. I also tell her where Steele fits in, the DVD he got and the things he had done to Josh. I tell her we are supposed to meet up with Clint Adams on Monday.

That night we talk for a long time and I feel so much closer to her. I am thankful for how she reacted and consoled me. We talk about how Dad being away impacts us, we both miss him. Eventually, we go to bed and I'm feeling a little bit better than before but drift off thinking of a song I once heard in the Wonder Years TV show when a teacher dies.

(Scan the QR code or hold down Ctrl and click the link)

https://www.youtube.com/watch?v=ZvZmWYE6RIw

Chapter 14

I talk to my parents about whether I should go to the funeral and maybe try to apologise to Josh's parents. They are adamant I should not go and they are insistent that I don't even try to contact them. I secretly wanted them to say that, but at the same time I also want to try to make things right and I know to do that I will need to eventually talk to his family, not so much for them, but for me. For now though I'm happy with my parents' decision, but it doesn't prevent me from thinking of Josh and what is happening at his funeral. I think of how his family must be feeling. I think of Taylor Harper and what the others are thinking of me right now. I have never felt this way before where my mood is so low. I have always been a confident person for as long as I can remember, not since I had that bullying incident when I was very young did I feel this vulnerable.

I start to think about the DVD Josh sent. He mentioned a couple of times that I wasn't that well liked and that others were just too scared to not treat me well. I think about that and the fact that everyone has treated me differently since Josh died. I expected some reaction, but no one has even tried to really talk to me. I haven't exactly been my chirpy self either but it's a very different environment and I am definitely feeling like an outsider. I don't like that feeling, I even preferred, at some weird level, Taylor's reaction rather than no one wanting to speak to me or talk behind my back and then when I get near, they stop talking. I start to feel a little sorry for myself and start to question the relationships I thought I had and worry that Josh is right when he says I'm not that well liked. I don't really know but I can't ignore what has been going on and these thoughts linger in my head and I analyse some of the behaviour of my classmates in my head over the last few days. There are definitely some who I would have expected a negative reaction from, but the ones that are a surprise are my own "friends" and the two Emily's who have been very friendly towards me. They have all "jumped off" and I can't ignore that. I try to convince myself that it is temporary given the sadness and shock that comes with an event like this.

I convince myself that even I have reacted to this event and not been myself, so maybe once the funeral is over and a little time goes by things will go back to normal. I think of an old Guns & Roses song called Don't Cry but when I check on YouTube, I find a cover by Karise Eden: *Don't Cry*:

(Scan the QR code or hold down Ctrl and click the link)

https://www.youtube.com/watch?v=T-i2q0HIkfE

I am feeling a bit sorry for myself and find myself crying a bit. It is a song saying not to cry and is saying I will feel better in the morning. I play the song a few times, I'm impressed by her version of the song and I feel a bit better as I think of the lyrics.

Chapter 15

I ask Clint to organise a meeting with Steele and his parents at the school, with the intent on exercising Josh's wish to help him change his behaviour. I feel a little more tense than I did the other day, I briefly fluctuate in my head between sadness, anger and a feeling of excitement that I am in control, but it's a lot harder to do to stay there than Clint suggests. Frankly, I'm plain scared, I don't like confrontations and I'm not sure how they will react. Clint warns me they could be super defensive, expecting we might be coming after Steele. He advised me that he had advised them of the letter Josh had given him and his conversations with me. He also said at first, they were very defensive that Steele had done nothing wrong, that maybe Josh just made this stuff up. He said he had expected that reaction, it's only natural for parents to protect their children, but once he outlined my intention and Josh's wishes for Steele, they seemed to be more open to this meeting.

Clint then met with Steele himself and said he immediately wanted the meeting. He indicated that since the DVD he got from Josh, the other student's reaction towards him and his own internal perception of the outcome, he doesn't know what to do and feels himself going down a spiral of depression and generally feeling bad. He says he doesn't know how, but he feels he needs to meet with me to help that process. His parents were supportive of him and after he left, they indicated that he was taking the whole thing very hard and they had concerns for him because he didn't know what to do. They said they were intending to wait a few weeks and see if time would help, but in the back of their minds they had considered sending him to a counsellor if the school's intended intervention did not help.

This makes me feel a little better about the meeting, the fact that this has hit him hard and that Clint has already assessed how they are feeling about things. I still grapple with the idea that this kid made a significant contribution to what happened to Josh. Working with Clint, he also made me realise that the "Experience-Mental Model" model he talks about in his sessions is where I realise that Josh's experience in dealing with bad news or bad experiences comes from me and my response to his dad leaving. My response was to spiral down into a very dark place. I guess that was the role model he had in terms of dealing with these things and as much as it makes me feel better to blame this kid, I have to be honest with myself and also make things right, because I am also a massive contributor to where Josh ended up.

I take on board what Clint has taught me, but it's not easy to confront yourself and say, 'You were not there for your own son!' I hadn't even considered what others think of me, but suddenly that adds pressure, which I did not need. It's weird when your thoughts actually put pressure on yourself. One of the great things Clint taught me was to assess my own thoughts and question them. I ask myself some questions like he told me to, to get myself in a "Blue Brain" space. I can't ignore the fact that I had an impact on Josh and his ultimate decision to take his own life, but I am different since I met Clint and I now have some tools I didn't have before. Tools that allow me to have that control over what I think. With this mind-set I feel more comfortable with having this meeting with Steele and his parents. I had thought of taking Rick with me for support, but for some reason, I choose to go alone. I need to do this for myself, I need to do this for my Josh.

Chapter 16

I talked to Clint Adams about meeting with Josh's mum, he advised of the letter Josh had sent him, which ties in with what he said in the DVD. At first, my parents were concerned that Clint and Josh's mum may be gunning to get me somehow, but when he explained the letter and what his mum's thoughts were, they felt more comfortable to have the meeting. I personally wanted to have some kind of talk to his mum for a few days now. I can't seem to let the feeling of guilt go away. That's the only label I can put to it. I constantly replay some of the things I did to Josh over and over in my head and I keep thinking of how he was feeling. I watched his DVD a number of times and it's like I have a constant pit in my stomach. On some occasions it gets so bad that I have to rush to the toilet and throw up.

I can't wait for this meeting, I'm not sure it will help, but I need to do something, this feeling just won't go away and I have no idea what to do to fix it. I start to think about what to say to her when we meet. I start to think about what she must think of me and that doesn't make me feel any better. I can only imagine the anger she might have towards me. As much as Clint indicated that she wanted to follow through with Josh's wishes to help me, I can't help but think about what her own thoughts might be. The loss would be great for her and knowing my involvement I'm sure she may not be as willing to forgive and forget as easy as that.

I know I want to have this meeting, but I'm also scared of what she will be thinking of me. My own guilt is killing me and I just can't keep doing what I'm doing because it's starting to take a toll. I find I'm not sleeping; I have been getting lots of mouth ulcers and headaches. I find that I'm not eating very well and don't really feel like doing anything. My parents can see it's having an impact. They have surprised me with how supportive they have been and how they have rallied to protect me, but even though that has been a positive, I still have these internal feelings that they can't help me with. I need to have this meeting to hopefully start a move to help me out of this hole I see myself in.

I need a distraction so I start to look up some stuff on YouTube, I'm liking Karise Eden's sound and I really liked her original song she sang in the *Voice* Final, she's pretty amazing. I play it a few times and I think it's sad and you can read that into the lyric that maybe she's had a tough life. I start to find myself thinking more about others' emotions and really looking deeper into things. I'm not sure that is good, but I somehow feel good about doing that. I listen to the song a few times and kind of want to protect her. It's like I would have wanted to prevent her from feeling so bad and prevented what happened to her to then write that song. I'm definitely not myself right now. I am surprised by my thinking.

Karise Eden: *I Was Your Girl*:

(Scan the QR code or hold down Ctrl and click the link)

https://www.youtube.com/watch?v=WBnlC1SRTYA

Chapter 17

It's finally the morning of the meeting, Clint has organised for us to meet in his office. I get there early to talk to him before Steele and his parents arrive. The "butterflies" in my stomach are working overtime, I'm highly anxious and a little scared of how I will react to them. My thoughts fluctuate between Josh's wishes and my anger towards Steele, my own guilt for not being able to help Josh and also sadness for my loss.

I sit with Clint and he talks me through the dialogue model, and reminds me that the key is to have what the model calls a "Blue Pool Conversation", where the conversation is free of fear and aggression.

(Scan the QR code or hold down Ctrl and click the link)

http://agilecoffee.com/toolkit/crucial-conversations/

It makes a lot of sense because when I think about someone pushing in line, I deliberately won't have that conversation because there is fear on my behalf. I fear that the person will react aggressively towards me or won't like me and I let my fear dictate my actions.

Talking through the model and just generally talking to him makes me feel a bit calmer. He makes me laugh, his energy and enthusiasm lifts my spirits and I "know" I can do this. I hear the office front door open and can see a tall young man and an older man and woman, obviously Steele and his family. My stomach does a couple of flips, but I remind myself to be strong. I also see that they aren't exactly looking super confident. I guess they don't really want to be here either. I look at Steele and I'm surprised by his physical presence compared to Josh who was significantly shorter and less muscular. I can see that Josh would not have stood much of a chance from a physical point of view in trying to defend himself from this boy.

I look at his face and our eyes lock briefly before he looks away. I can tell he is feeling very uncomfortable and even though I have all these mixed emotions running inside me, I naturally put out my hand to shake his and introduce myself. My "natural niceness" comes out and I remind myself of Josh's wishes and Clint's reminder of a Blue Pool Conversation. I can't allow myself to become aggressive or defensive, so I can't yell at this kid because then he could become aggressive or defensive. I need to help create the safety for the conversation and let's just have a productive conversation. I see he is defensive and his parents look tense as they each introduce themselves to me and shake my hand.

Clint shakes their hands as well as a greeting as he met with them recently. He then sits us all down, I feel a little outnumbered on my side of the table looking across at the three of them, but then Clint sits next to me and I don't feel so bad. He explains that the purpose of today is to get things out in the open and that we all will need to be on alert for anyone getting aggressive or defensive. If anyone sees that happening even in themselves, then they call a timeout while we discuss why that is happening, so we can go back to the Blue Pool Conversation.

He turns to Steele and asks him to start off. He finds it hard to look me in the eye for anything more than a second or so. He starts off by saying how sorry he is for my loss and then goes on to explain how hard this has hit him and how sorry he is for how he treated Josh. I impress myself by not getting angry while he speaks and I take it all in. I can see genuine remorse in his face, his parents don't say anything, and we all just let him get it off his chest.

He starts to cry during the process and says he knows he can't fix this and take back what has been done but wants to do something to make amends. He says he doesn't know what that is but wants to do something. He stops, I can tell the emotion has got the better of him, and as bizarre as it sounds, I start to feel sorry for him. I watch him intently and I can tell this has been tough on him, I can tell the remorse is there and also that his intent was not for this to happen. I think I should explore this further and ask him questions about why he chose to do those things to Josh?

He says he's not entirely sure, except that there were things about Josh which he says drew his attention for the wrong reasons, like wanting to wear '80s' clothes and the fact that other kids thought he was a little weird. He says it made it easier to make fun of Josh because others were supporting it by laughing and the fact that no one was really supporting Josh and telling him to stop. He indicated that he knows that it is wrong upon reflection but at the time he hadn't considered the impact it was having on Josh. He says that he wishes he could take what he did back and he starts to cry, and I mean CRY, he starts to sob uncontrollably and his parents hug him and try to console him. Clint says we should take a break and they leave the office and go for a walk.

I stay with Clint and we talk about how I think it's going. I explain that I still feel in control, I'm happy that he seems to have really thought about the impact of his actions. I'm also a little surprised with the significance of the impact this has had on him. I had expected some cocky, arrogant kid who was going to come here to protect himself and come here to try and stop me from taking the matter further. Instead what I have seen is someone who is clearly finding it hard to deal with the fact that they have some responsibility for the death of another human being and they don't know how to deal with that.

I find myself feeling greater empathy for Steele, because I feel the same way. I am also responsible for the death of Josh, it's more my inaction which has contributed to it. I also don't know how to deal with that.

When they return, Steele has controlled himself, his eyes are red from crying and I suspect his mother has been crying too. I start to talk and pour out my heart, going through how my first marriage breakdown impacted me and Josh, how I was not as aware as I should have been about things happening at school. As I talk through Rick's impact on Josh, I suddenly realise I really couldn't bring Rick to this meeting, because my relationship with Rick and his relationship with Josh also contributed to Josh not wanting to talk about things. Rick would tell Josh to suck things up and say that it was character building to have some adversity in his life.

I guess upon reflection this prevented Josh from talking about things with Rick and me. He would have felt that Rick would think he was a cry-baby if he brought it up, so he suffered in silence hiding the impact this stuff was happening. This realisation hits me quite hard and I can tell that everyone in the room understands this and tries to console me, but I'm crying a lot now. It is emotional; I do exactly what Steele did and Clint calls another break.

The break is a welcome relief. I walk outside and I half expected Clint to follow me, but I guess he read that it is better for me to be alone right now and I silently thank him for that. I try to talk myself into Blue Brain, but the thought keeps coming back that my relationship with Rick has had a significant impact on where Josh ended up and my inability to see the effects it was having on him meant I didn't actively do anything to get him to the point that he opened up. I think of the Dialogue model and piece it together for Josh. He saw or heard something, he told himself a story, he felt a certain way and then he acted. His action was to go to silence because what he saw and heard was Rick telling him to toughen up and underlying that he could have also picked up that Rick wasn't interested in helping him. I don't believe that was Rick's intention, but I can see how Josh may have made that assumption. This then meant he probably felt rejected which meant he didn't want to have the conversation with us again as he didn't feel safe to have it. When I say safe, it was he didn't feel safe that Rick wouldn't react the same way and call him a woos or to suck it up. The dialogue model is so simple and I can see that it shows our patterns of behaviour and certain thoughts.

I deliberately force myself to tell myself a different story and turn my focus to what I can do to prevent this from happening to another family. True to form the technique calms me and I'm in Blue Brain again, ready to find a solution for the problem rather than concentrating on the problem itself.

I return to the office and our conversation turns to, 'Where to from here?' Steele goes first and says he's not sure what to do but he wants to be able to do something to either spread awareness to make sure this doesn't happen again. He asks Clint if he would help him do that. Clint says he is happy to work with him to do that. His parents indicate they want to support Steele in any way to help him do that, they also ask if Clint would be doing any kind of therapy to help Steele cope because they indicate that he is struggling and they have genuine concerns that if left unaddressed could lead to bigger long-term problems. Clint indicates that the process should address helping him and also focus on helping others in the school.

The Connors family leave and it's just me and Clint. He asks me how I'm feeling. I realise I got through the meeting and without feeling anger. I definitely felt sadness and a little bit of guilt, but I never once directed anger at Steele. Anyone else would have wanted to see him suffer and their natural tendency would be for vengeance, but my Red Brain / Blue Brain training helped me prepare myself mentally. I didn't realise it could be that easy, especially given what has happened. I am amazed how asking questions of yourself does change which area of the brain is being used and if used well enough can change which direction you go.

Clint and I talk for a while and I realise how far I have come in a few days. I ask him how things went from his point of view with Steele and his family, but he throws back to me and asks, 'What was going to be your best outcome before you went in?'

I think about that for a second and I say, 'I just didn't want a confrontation, but I also wanted them to acknowledge that Steele did the wrong thing and although he can't change the result, he wants to make things better.' I also wanted the outcome to be that I could be strong and if Josh was looking down, he would feel some form of pride that I could do it. Clearly, he had some doubts I could do it and to his credit, he involved Clint to give me a hand. Saying this to Clint makes me realise I answered my own question. I feel some pride in that moment.

I ask Clint where we go from here and he tells me he intends to run some sessions with all the students at the school and also give the teachers some strategies to play their part. He also mentions that he has a specific one on one plan with Steele, to help him deal with his demons and also to assist him to make things better. I feel happy that we are looking to a solution, I feel energised despite how much today, and the preceding days of worrying about today took out of me. I go home and just put on some music to chill and relax.

Passenger: *Let Her Go*:

(Scan the QR code or hold down Ctrl and click the link)

http://www.youtube.com/watch?v=RBumgq5yVrA

Chapter 18

My name is Clint Adams, born in South Africa, I was a good student, lots of friends over there and immigrated over here to Australia in 1984 at the age of almost 13. I was bullied in my first couple of years at school here, little things like having shit hung on my South African accent, or even just standing up in class to answer a teacher's question, which was drilled into you in South Africa, but here it was simply another thing for them to pick on. There was one guy in particular who would play up for everyone and I was his point of attention so he could get a laugh. Of course, I was smaller than him and he was physically well endowed. I had a few run ins with him, but I was lucky I had a few friends who looked out for me and one of them even broke this guy's ankle and that seemed to slow him down. I also would fight back and remember throwing a ceramic bowl at this guy's head in a home economics class. I suppose this experience many years ago led me to a point where I always wanted to help people who were struggling.

After I left high school, I studied psychology and I joined the Police force, probably more out of necessity to get money than actively wanting to help anyone, but it did expose me to a wide variety of people. People doing it tough, people having lost someone in an accident or a murder or even a child in a SIDS death. There are people who had their possessions stolen or who had been assaulted, raped even kidnapped. People can do horrible things to other people. When you compare us to other countries, we seem so much better off, but then being a cop here exposes you to more, and you see we still do these things. It may not be as often but it still happens. We take our good government for granted, no one seems to appreciate what a good government can do.

I had a life-changing event when I was working the police cells. We all had to do three months in the cells looking after prisoners waiting to either go to court, or had been to court and sentenced and were waiting to go to prison. We had three exercise yards and each yard had four cells attached to it. There were always more male than female prisoners. On one occasion we had only one woman in the cells, I won't mention her name, but she was about 25 years old and because she was alone in the cells, I would spend a bit of time talking to her. I found out she had been in trouble before and was sentenced to three years this time. She was a heroin addict and her habit had led her to commit a number of crimes to support her drug use.

I also found out she had a young daughter, who her parents were looking after while she was going to be in prison. She was very emotional, time in the cells has meant she was coming off the drugs and reality was something she couldn't escape or mask with substances in there. She was depressed and felt that she had hit rock bottom and couldn't see a way out. We talked about what brought her to this point. She fell in with the wrong crowd, started using drugs and escalated up the drug scale and heroin brought her here.

Over a few days we had a number of conversations and I remember saying to her that this was an opportunity. If she wanted to be a part of her daughter's life, things needed to change, that she needed to use the time in prison to ask herself what she really wanted and once she knew that she could set her course. I remember quoting to her a part in Alice in Wonderland, where Alice comes to a fork in the road and asks the Cheshire cat which way she should go? The cat replies, 'Where do you want to go?'

Alice replies, 'I don't know.'

The cat replies, 'Well, then it doesn't matter.' In a nutshell if you don't know where you want to go, you can't really plan the trip. You just end up where you do.

We talked over a few days about what she really wanted and she said she wanted to get her daughter back. We discussed what she needed to do to accomplish that. She said she needed to stay off drugs, do everything right in prison so she could get an early release. I could see a change in her face and one day I came in to work and found they had moved her to prison. I never really thought that much about her after that.

A couple of years later, I was running a path I ran quite regularly, and I saw a woman come running out of a house waving violently to catch my attention. I stopped and looked at her and I recognised this same woman, who looked a lot healthier. She said she had seen me run past a few times and thought it was me, given my ethnic look I guess I stand out a bit more. She said she wanted to stop me to thank me for the time I spent with her and the things I had said to her. She indicated when she was being taken to prison, she kept asking herself where she wanted to go and she kept answering "home to my baby girl". She said once she knew where, she was resolute about that and did what was required to achieve it. She said she was released early and although she was living with her parents now, she was being a mother to her daughter and has not used heroin since. She said she just wanted to stop me to say thank you and gave me a hug.

As I ran off, I was choked up with emotion, I had finally made a significant difference in someone's life and it changed the course of my career. I ended up studying Rehabilitation counselling and eventually left the police force to work as an Injury Management Consultant, which gave me great exposure to people who had been having lots of trouble dealing with either physical injuries or psychological issues like bullying and harassment type problems and stress related issues. Through this work I became fascinated with why some people who had significant injuries could come out the other end with an absolutely fantastic attitude and get on with life, while others with seemingly less significant injuries would struggle through their lives, leading to depression, broken relationships, substance abuse, obesity and many other issues. Through discussions with them there were some common themes, their focus was the biggest. The ones who focused on what they were losing or had lost seemed to do it the toughest. The ones who focused on what else they could do, basically would not allow themselves to feel sorry for themselves, these seemed to be the most resilient.

It was out of this work that I started researching what was physically happening in a person's body when certain things happened. There is lots of information showing certain patterns, certain relationships between conditions like depression and physical components like serotonin levels and how although they don't know which causes which, they go hand in hand. I love reading and Tony Robbins is an excellent source of information. He is great at giving you a good perspective on things.

(Scan the QR code or hold down Ctrl and click the link)

https://www.youtube.com/results?search_query=tony+robbins+motivation

If you want to learn more about some of these things, check out some of his books; they are insightful. My view is if you are in one of these states, but if you want to find out more, that is always a good step, because it is focused on a "blue brain" experience.

Chapter 19

As much as my meeting with the Connors' family went well, I still have these waves of emotion and I do catch myself a few times and try the techniques of Red Brain/Blue Brain but it keeps coming back. I decide to call Clint and see what he thinks, I somehow feel he can help me, he seems to know this stuff and probably it has something to do with Josh "choosing" him to be the person that could help me. This makes me feel comfortable to ask him.

He agrees to meet with me that day and I go to see him at his office. I get to meet his wife Heidi who is also his secretary and she is a statuesque blonde with the most inviting manner. She is so friendly I could see myself being friends with her. I go into Clint's office and explain to him that I'm so up and down with my thoughts. I know I'm not spiralling downward like I did when my ex-husband left, but I can't seem to shake this feeling. He surprises me when he indicates that he believes it's because I haven't actually grieved Josh's death yet. I explain that Josh didn't want me to do that, that he wanted me to be strong and not let my emotions get the better of me like it did last time. Clint gets up and gets a book from his rather large book filled shelves and hands it to me it's called *Secrets of a Bulletproof Spirit* by Jillian Quinn and Azim Khamisa.

(Scan the QR code or hold down Ctrl and click the link)

https://www.amazon.com/Secrets-Bulletproof-Spirit-Bounce-Hardest/dp/0345506030

He explains to me that you can't will a serious loss away without dealing with it. He says grieving is part of the healing process, just distracting yourself won't help heal. Even though the distraction might be positive and you try to catch your negative thoughts and try to put yourself in a Blue Brain space, you will fluctuate between the two because it is still bubbling underneath unresolved. He points out that last time I may have grieved in a way that was detrimental to me, he indicates that there are better ways to grieve and this book will help me look at that differently.

He asks me what the plan with Steele is. I'm not really prepared for that; I had been happy with where it ended but hadn't really considered the "what next". I ask him what he thinks I should do, but true to his way of doing things, he says that it's not his job to tell me what to do, but he asks me, 'Where do you want to get to with this?' I'm not really sure how to answer that, I guess I want my son back, but that's not going to happen. The emotion hits me again and I start to think I really want the Connors' family to suffer, but I realise that won't help me, that it won't bring Josh back, but it might make me feel better for a short time. I impress myself that I "catch" myself going into Red Brain again and deliberately change my focus. I can see Clint acknowledging my progress with a little smile and I feel proud of myself.

Clint quotes something from Alice in Wonderland. I can't recall the exact words, but it goes something like this, Alice comes to a fork in the road and sees the Cheshire cat in a tree and she asks it which way she should go? It asks, 'Where do you want to go?'

She says, 'I don't know.'

He then replies, 'Well then, it doesn't matter.' He proceeds to explain that until I know where I want this to end, I will just float in a direction, maybe good, maybe bad, but if I actually know where I want to go with this, I can start being deliberate about making it happen. He explains that "Intent" is the key. It makes a lot of sense but I still don't know where I'm taking it and I hadn't fully worked out any true intent. He advises me to read the book and ask myself the question what is going to be best for me? I leave after another conversation with Heidi on my way out, with my book under my arm.

I go home and start to read. The book is very insightful it definitely gives me insight in terms of "how" I grieved last time, but it also gives insight that I really haven't grieved for my loss of Josh. I understand Clint's point about me distracting myself, which in a way is me running from facing that loss. The authors of the book understand that our culture tends to "frown" upon grieving, no one really teaches us how to do that better, or even that it is part of a healing process. The book is great as it explains we all take "hits" in our lives and just thinking positive and "cheering" ourselves up doesn't help in the long run.

I love the concept in the book of allocating a grieving period. It talks about various religions doing this as part of their ritual, some grieve 40 days some seven days, but there is a grieving period and it is a finite time. The book is just what I needed, it has a section in each chapter called "Bounce Back Bootcamp" which include practical things you can do to do exactly that, which is Bounce Back when you've taken a HIT. I read it from cover to cover and can't help but feel I'm going to get through this. I cry a little though when I think that it took Josh's death to help me get stronger, and he has led me to the person who knows what I need, and I can't explain the bittersweet feeling that gives me. I fluctuate between giggling like a school girl, even though hot tears roll down my cheeks, it's the weirdest feeling, but it's positive, so positive that I want to listen to something uplifting and a song springs to mind, Ludacris: *Rest of My Life*:

(Scan the QR code or hold down Ctrl and click the link)

http://www.youtube.com/watch?v=J_nziODUGcw

It seems appropriate as the lyrics suggest I'm on a journey and things are starting to roll my way, I feel amazing. I rethink about what Clint and the stupid cat asked, 'Where do you want to go?' I have an answer now and this excites me. I have my plan, my "Alice" Roadmap. I'm on a journey I'm on a roll! I sleep brilliantly that night and the next day I call my parents and my closest friends to organise a meeting to advise them and Rick of my plan.

The next day they all meet at my house and I explain to them a summary of what the book has taught me and as a result I plan to have a 14-day grieving period. I explain to them that in this period I will need their help and support as I will not be taking care of myself, I will need them to prepare my meals, deflect calls and others outside this room away from me. I explain I will be immersing myself in feeling sad, nostalgic and I will be looking at anything that reminds me of Josh, I will watch movies that make me sad and cry more. I emphasise that I DO NOT want any of them to try to cheer me up or offer any words of comfort as I need to grieve and celebrate my son's brief life. I tell them that no matter how bad I look, I don't want anyone to comment to me on what I look like or if I choose not to eat or do something they don't approve of, just to hold those thoughts for the two weeks and let me be. I ask a commitment from them and they all agree. I turn to Rick and let him know this will be tougher on him as he is here 24/7 and he will need to take care of Georgia on his own, but the others all chime in that they can share having Georgia for the two weeks and if Rick wants to, he can come and spend time with them temporarily, plus Rick's parents have a holiday house a few hours away and he says he can always go there for a few days at a time.

So it's all set, I start my grieving period tomorrow and I actually look forward to it, because since I found Josh on that night, I have been carrying this weight and not really reflected on my time with Josh. I have a positive feeling about this, even though I know the next two weeks is going to involve a lot of pain, and me deliberately seeking it. I think about my experience when my first husband left, I had a grieving period then, only it was not planned, and I was so caught up in the anger, the bitterness, the trying to get him back that I never really dealt with the issue. I never really grieved, I recognise now that I pretty much moved on accidently and I never really forgave my ex. The book talks about forgiveness, and I never really considered that forgiveness is less about the person you are forgiving, and more about you not feeling anger and even hatred towards that person, and the effects that has on you.

I'm fascinated by this notion that my ex doesn't even need to know that I forgive him, that I can simply "decide" to do it and it could change how I feel about him from then on and how I feel in general. Truth be told, every time I think about this, there is a "twist of a knife" feeling, even though I'm happily married now and have started another family with Rick, I still hold a lot of resentment for Josh's dad. Knowing what I now know from Clint's Red Brain information, I have a lot of emotional memories, not necessarily positive with him and when I think of him, I get my Red Brain going, which is anger and sadness, probably more anger now than sadness, but it's still there. I re-read the "Forgiveness" Bounce back Bootcamp, while I know this is my grieving period coming up, I also know that there is some work I need to do to forgive Josh, because I haven't really dealt with the fact that he took his own life and it's something I know I want to deal with in the next two weeks. As much as it's empowering, I still have that fear that I may not be strong enough to really confront this. I don't want to let Josh down again. He was specific to Clint and me that he worried about my ability to deal with this. I feel better equipped because of the things Clint and the book have taught me, I also know I have the support of Clint and my friends and family, because I have actively asked for it this time. The one thing the book specifies is not to put too much on your family and friends, because they have their own things to do, and also, they may not know anything about this, so use them sparingly. I am happy to ask my family and friends to help me with looking after my daughter, making me food and the basics, I know I need Clint as my counsellor to get me through this. I am deliberate in my head to make sure I don't put too much on the others.

I don't sleep that well tonight, I feel like someone going into a big game, a little excited, but also scared of failure, but all the while knowing the prize is big. My "Alice" roadmap is based on the destination I have set for myself, which is to properly grieve Josh, his life, my life with him and also to honour his wish of making things different for others. My other destination is to forgive my ex-husband so I can move on. I realise that all the negativity I have towards him is in my own hands, how I think about him is actually up to me. I give him more power and hold over me, even though I haven't seen him or even spoke to him in years. I actually laugh at myself when I think of how obvious it should be that I am causing myself that pain, not him. The book indicates that Nelson Mandela equates this to: "Taking poison and hoping someone else will die." The effects are all mine, me hating and resenting him means nothing to him and keeps affecting me, why would I do that to myself? It was a "hit", I never let the wound heal. I was always picking at it and making it worse for myself. I should have looked after myself and allowed myself to heal. I should have grieved better for that loss and got out the other end. I'm still here and I can change that, starting tomorrow. I feel better and drift off to sleep.

The next morning Rick tells me that he has organised for meals to be delivered for me for the next three days. He and Georgia are going up to his parents' holiday house. He tells me that he, my parents and friends all got together after our meeting and decided the first three days should be alone. They drew up a contact roster that meant someone was always contactable when I needed them and they would "come a running". I thank him and wave him and Georgia goodbye as they pull out of the driveway. I go back inside and realise for the first time that I have not been alone in my house since I found Josh. The wave of emotion is sudden. I think of those events and me trying to get him down, the fear is enormous, I was so scared that he was dead and I try to break the cycle of thinking about this events, but I "decide" to let it happen and actively replay the night as it unfolded.

I am deliberately focusing on my thinking as I replay the events, I sort of press pause as I step through the events and think about what I was feeling and saying to myself as it happens. I find myself picking up the "Red Brain" responses as you would expect, with my son hanging from the roof. I find that I can re-experience the feelings, but can step outside myself a bit and just think about my thoughts. I understand now when Clint says our thoughts can sometimes be actions and sometimes be automatic. The difference is all in me, consciously thinking about my thinking and deliberately doing that. It's the same thoughts, but the consciousness changes it from being automatic and following an automatic path to being automatic and taking a conscious path.

Knowing what I know now, I can see why I struggled so much last time, every time I thought about my ex, I would have the automatic response and feel either anger or sadness and would stay there for long periods of time. If I knew then what I now know, I would be deliberately challenging my thoughts more and working to change the path my thoughts continued on. I keep working my way through that night and pay close attention to my thoughts and also how I'm feeling and especially my own self talk. I take a lot of notes.

This takes a few hours and I am a little bit tired. I realise I had not told Clint about my plan and give him a buzz, but it automatically gets diverted and goes to his secretary and wife, Heidi. As I said before, I find her very easy to talk to and feel comfortable telling her the plan and to pass that on to Clint. She surprises me a little as she starts to open up and explains that she understands the grieving process as she also had Clint explain this process to her when she also had unresolved issues with her stepfather stemming back many years when her stepfather was a drunk and when her mother wasn't around he would say nasty things to her. Things like she was a piece of crap and a no hoper and told her that she was trash and he was glad he didn't have his own children. When she was explaining this to me, I can tell she was getting quite emotional.

She explained how that changed her teenage years, as her mother never got to witness this type of comments, he was careful to make sure she was not home when he would say these things, and this was a very bad dynamic in the house. She said she would deliberately try to be out of the house when she was likely to be alone with him. Heidi said that for many years she felt like she wasn't worthy of love, that somehow, she had done something wrong, which was why he said she was trash. She went further by saying how her distrust of men nearly cost her the relationship with Clint. However, she also pointed out that Clint's behaviour didn't help that and probably amplified her reactions in the early years.

Clint is a very outgoing person and by his own admission is a "show pony" who likes to be the centre of attention. She says Clint also admits that he realised that he was a person who was ego driven, in the sense that he always needed others' approval to feel good about himself. He would seek out that type of approval, so would flirt with other women, would make himself the centre of attention, because he is naturally funny and gets that perceived approval from others when they laugh at his jokes and his stories.

She said that it wasn't until they had a massive fight that he realised the impact he was having on her when he was doing these things. It opened up a lot of self-exploration for both of them. He explained the grieving process to her, which was part of her healing with her stepfather. While she admits she hasn't contacted him, she has forgiven him, for her benefit, not his and actually feels sorry for him because he has missed out on so many things with his step-kids and grandkids. She says she still feels sadness when she thinks about what could have been, but she also has a greater appreciation for her own strength and how it has galvanised her relationship with Clint.

She says for a long time there was a pattern of arguments with Clint, where she would accuse him of cheating or flirting with someone else and of course he would deny it. She admits that looking back it was only evidence of flirting, but she was able to convince herself that he was doing more and this would lead to big arguments. His flirting and her lack of trust of men led to problems and unless they dealt with it, it was going to continue. She says that when she had big arguments with him, she would then feel bad and worry that he would then leave her. She would go overboard to try to make things right, but then underneath it all still resent his behaviour and him, and then she would feel like she had let herself down and her self-worth would take a hit. She says it wasn't until she went to the root cause that she realised how it impacted so many other aspects of her life. Her forgiving her stepdad had led her to release that feeling of anger and resentment.

I thank her for sharing these personal details and hang up feeling somehow better even though I'm supposed to be in a grieving period. I decide to replay the DVD they played at Josh's funeral and I sit and watch it by myself with a cup of tea and the best biscuits in the world, the Tim Tam. I watch the photos go across the screen and listening to the music he chose makes me cry, I don't feel guilty or bad that I am sad, I actually feel the pain, but also feel the celebration that was his life. It's a very different experience than last time, I actually am in control, I am sad and there is pain, a lot of pain, but there is also a great feeling of nostalgic moments and the photos invoke trips down memory lane, when we had a lot of fun with Josh. I see Christmas photos of yesteryear, holiday pictures when we would go snowboarding and swim at the beaches.

I cry uncontrollably until my stomach starts to ache and the tears appear to have evaporated, I find myself laughing a lot as well, just seeing him in his school uniform for the first time, was like taking me straight there that day. The smell, the feeling, it all floods my senses. I feel the pain and I'm also feeling the joy, it's very difficult to describe I cry and laugh myself to sleep and I REALLY sleep.

Chapter 20

I'm feeling better after the meeting with Josh's mum, I feel that some progress was made, for me in my own head anyway. I start to analyse the way the conversations went, and I didn't really pick up any major negative feelings towards me from her. I talk to my parents in the car on the way back from the meeting and they confirm the same thoughts as me that it went well considering the circumstances. I have a couple of days off school by agreement with the principal, but I actually regret that request as I sort of want to get back to school and try to get back to normal, but at the same time, I'm also a little anxious about how others are considering my involvement. I check my Facebook and across the group there is an unusual silence about the whole thing. I don't know if it's still shock or something else.

I get home and decide to surf the net a bit, I get on YouTube and start thinking about "Change", a number of songs and articles pop up. I start checking out some of them, my favourites include,

John Mayer: *Waiting on a World to Change*:

(Scan the QR code or hold down Ctrl and click the link)

http://www.youtube.com/watch?v=oBIxScJ5rlY

Tracy Chapman: *Change*:

https://www.youtube.com/watch?v=bukXKdzyGEY

Scorpions: *Wind of Change*:

http://www.youtube.com/watch?v=n4RjJKxsamQ

While the others have a bit more meaning about change, this one is a bit funky and the girl is pretty hot.

Hyuna Kim: *Change*:

https://www.youtube.com/watch?v=G6JppjQSTh8

I decide to ring Clint Adams to see how he thought things went and what he thinks the next steps should be, I find him to be very helpful and to be someone I feel most comfortable with. My parents also commented on how much they thought he was helpful. My dad also recalls Clint coming to do some team things at his steel mill with really good overall results. I give him a call and he answers with what I can only describe as a happy attitude, I can literally feel that he has a smile on his face as he answers the call. I identify myself and he asks me how I think things went. I reply that my parents and I all thought it went well. I ask him how Mrs McKenzie was after we left. He indicates that he and she agreed that it went very well, but that it was only first steps for both parties.

We discuss the where-to-from-here part for me. Clint indicates that he has a plan for the school, which focuses on dealing with Josh's death, but also one which is aimed at prevention in the future which is a bigger piece of work aimed at the teachers. He suggests to me to read certain books he has at his office and I organise to meet him in the morning to pick them up.

Chapter 21

Clint calls me and advises me that Josh's mother had a meeting with Steele and his parents. He says it appeared to go well and he is working with both of them to help deal with the impact of Josh's suicide. He says he would like to talk to me about the program that he was intending to run at the school. He says he thinks we should revise the rollout and to fast track its introduction to Josh's year level, as he believes it could help that group to deal with some of the issues. I agree to meet in my office later that day.

Clint turns up, happy and joking as always and he starts to step me through the program. In a nutshell he says he would still run his program of Red Brain / Blue Brain with my teachers and get them to give each other feedback to help them develop a better working relationship. He says he had been thinking about what to do with the students and came up with a program, which actually takes into account the same principles of the Teachers' Program, but can actually help the students to learn what Clint says is enabling behaviour. He says the key is for the teachers to understand the principles and then apply it themselves to develop "lessons" for their students like they would with any curriculum. He likens it to a "train the trainer" type system and then the trainers develop the content to help the students once they understand the principles.

The idea has merit and Clint talks me through the nitty-gritty of it, he hands me his actual proposal.

After he leaves, I read through the proposal and feel true excitement that this program could be an absolute game changer for our education system. I got into teaching because I wanted to have an influence on children's and teenagers' lives and wanted to see my students go on to make great contributions in the wide world. I loved being a teacher, I loved seeing how they progress over the years, but I also always saw bullying at schools and it only seemed to get worse. No one really helped us with dealing with that. We would simply punish those who were either caught or who had been "dobbed in" by others, but this was never that effective. Clint's program aims at helping teachers and students to do things in a different way. He gets the students to analyse their thoughts and also gets teachers to facilitate and set up opportunities for them to have conversations with their schoolmates early on in the learning process, so that they can actually learn to create their own team and group culture. The aim is also to help them develop personal resilience and skills to deal with relationships in a more positive way.

The more I think about it, the more I can't believe we hadn't done this before. It's actually a lot simpler when you actually think about it, I see the possibilities and believe that it can make a difference in our education process, in a positive way. I also see how it could have an impact on other areas too, such as healthcare and even crimes. I re-read the proposal and feel even more confident that if all teachers and our education decision makers knew about this, they would be banging down the doors of our politicians and screaming for funding to make it happen. I know I'm going to. With that thought I start to ask myself some questions on what else I can do to enhance this process? Clint also gave me a book by Tony Robbins, which is actually a really big book, but told me to read the chapter based on questions. The book is the *Awaken the Giant Within*. I read the chapter, which walks you down a path of how powerful questions are and when you ask the right ones it can change your focus and it prompts me to ask questions of myself.

Awaken the Giant Within: By Tony Robbins.

(Scan the QR code or hold down Ctrl and click the link)

https://www.booktopia.com.au/awaken-the-giant-within-anthony-robbins/prod9781471167515.html?source=pla&gclid=CjwKCAiAhfzSBRBTEiwA N-ysWPY3dPvB-xz-

I feel my energy lifting, I realise I have been "coasting" in my role as Principal, resigned to the fact that each year we will lose a certain number of students and that only a certain number will succeed, we reached a ceiling of achievement and that's the best I could hope for. I tried to convince myself that this was OK, but underneath the 18-year-old wannabe teacher feels disappointed, I had a fresh enthusiasm that I could change the world, that I could influence young lives and make them want to learn and have a thirst for knowledge. I have seen students just like that on my journey, but the unfortunate part is I saw more do the opposite. I know we haven't got it right. Many people in our Education Club say that it is not our jobs to do the parents' job and I always thought we really can't have a big influence if the parents don't care. I often see patterns of the same thing over and over, where parents don't give their kids enough attention and they end up being bad students, who cause lots of issues to the other students. I can predict with a high degree of success, who will and won't make it based on this pattern.

What I love about this program is that it brings a certain rigour to us as teachers helping all kids to do what good parents do. I think we never really went to what Clint calls "Root cause analysis" of these students' behaviour. We were always so focused on teaching our curriculum, which is Maths, English, Science and the like to really notice and even think about why these kids would rock up at school with less understanding and not actually help them work on themselves while we educate on the subjects. When I think about what this program is suggesting, I feel a little embarrassed because Clint was coming here to help my team work better together and with Josh's death, I asked him to see if we could help the students and it literally took him days to come up with the program and it's ingeniously simple.

I go to bed with a warm and fuzzy feeling in my belly and it's very exciting. It's not often someone can reinvigorate your dreams, when for a lot of years the results of the education model were confirming that you would lose more than you could get through. I keep saying that this was as good as we can do. Don't get me wrong, my school and our teachers work very hard and we get results, but with this new strategy I really think we can change what we have always got. It's an amazing feeling to see the possibilities and KNOW it is a game changer. I hate the fact that it is so simple but love the fact that I asked the right question of the right person at the right time and I am going to be a big part of this journey.

I know that Clint realises the ramifications as do I, and I also know he will need to convince the right people to make this work across education, but I also know I am in control of my school and this is great for me. Old habits die hard its important work, but there will always be those who don't like new ideas. I ask myself questions about how I can help this along, it's got to be work that happens and I don't want Clint to just help my team, when I know he can help all my students and future students. I feel like my GIANT within has been awakened and he won't do nothing. I start thinking about how we promote this. I think of various methods, but my favourite is to do it and put the runs on the board at my own school and then pitch it rather than take it to the heads of education with just our speculation of what it can do.

I'm actually quite pumped and decide to listen to a song by Michael Jackson which takes me back to my idealistic views as a teacher to actually be able to heal the world.

Heal the world:

(Scan the QR code or hold down Ctrl and click the link)

http://www.youtube.com/watch?v=BWf-eARnf6U

I can't help but smile to myself, this idea has given me options I had never considered and now that I know I can't "un-know". The possibilities keep bouncing in my head and I find it very difficult to sleep, because for a long time I have not even thought in a proactive way.

Chapter 22

I catch up with Steele and give him a book to read. *The Decisive Moment: How the Brain Makes Up Its Mind* by Jonah Lehrer.

(Scan the QR code or hold down Ctrl and click the link)

http://www.amazon.co.uk/Decisive-Moment-Brain-Makes-Mind/dp/1847673155

I also instruct him to check out Jonah doing a speech on the content of the book, which is also quite informative.

http://www.youtube.com/watch?v=k4YsTDHuLTg

I explain to him that this book is to help him have a better understanding of what is happening in his head and why we make some of the decisions we make. I ask him to start a "thoughts diary". In it I instruct him to write down his thoughts that pop into his head for a period of a week and each night to write next to the thought whether it was positive or negative. I am doing this for him to gain some more awareness of his thoughts and then reflect on them later. It requires him to use Blue Brain to do the analysis, which actually also reverses some of the Red Brain responses as the Blue Brain requires more blood to do this analysis, so blood actually pumps from the muscles back into the brain. I also instruct him to set aside 30 minutes of each day to reflect on some of his actions at school and think about what thoughts that invokes and then to write them down in the diary as well.

My theory is that if we can at least be aware of ourselves, we can make changes accordingly. Often, we have formed patterns of thinking, which leads to how we feel and ultimately how we act, and this can often be negative or destructive patterns. There are some theories out there, based on an experiment done at Stanford University:

(Scan the QR code or hold down Ctrl and click the link)

http://en.wikipedia.org/wiki/Stanford_marshmallow_experiment

    It shows a correlation between how long children can delay gratification/show more self-control and their future success. This is a simplistic view but I personally think that thinking about our thoughts and delaying our natural reaction in some instances will help us make better choices. I like what Jonah says in the clip when being questioned, that sometimes we need to trust our emotions but sometimes we need to analyse the feeling and that can lead to making better decisions. I also found it interesting when he was talking about the monkey experiments which showed that "status or class" hierarchies lead to developmental problems with unborn babies. This really has some serious ramifications because it could explain some of the issues regarding those in lower socio-economic groups and how they differ to those who are in the higher socioeconomic groups.

    Steele and I talk for a while and he indicates that he will do as I have requested and then leaves. I call Vicki but she doesn't answer, it's been a few days into her grieving period, but I thought I would check on how she is going, I'm actually glad to have the phone ring out.

Chapter 23

I'm four days into my grieving period and I'm surprised by my thoughts through this process. I have focussed so heavily on Josh's life and also my loss that I expected to feel a lot worse, but I actually feel OK, not fantastic or happy, but OK. I have been deliberate in what I have been doing, I have some control this time and I feel an inner pride in myself for it. Rick and my friends and parents have all been fantastic. They have deflected things from me, they cook and clean and get out and leave me alone, but I also still have a tinge of missing my daughter, but I resist my urge to want to spend too much time dwelling on this. This is my Josh and me time, but I recheck that thought and realise this is my "Me" and my "Mind" time.

It's me and my thoughts and I have never thought about it that much in the past. Since meeting Clint I have realised that my thoughts and my internal dialogue with myself have led me to feel a certain way and then this leads to habitual feelings that have been very destructive for me. I also think that this has been destructive for Josh, because he would see the path it took me down and it taught him bad thinking patterns and habits, and it also meant he knew he couldn't rely on me. This thought alone starts making me feel sad, but I interrupt that thought and ask myself a "Blue Brain" question, as Clint puts it, and I start to think of what I can do for Georgia and myself and other children out there to make sure no one else has this problem.

I have worked my way through the book Clint gave me and found it very helpful about really being deliberate about my grief and not feeling embarrassed or rushed to get over it. I give Clint a call just to see if he has anything else, I should read that he thinks would help me. I tell him I really want to do something for other kids and parents that can help them not go through this. He suggests a couple and he drops it off to me later that day.

The first one is, *The Power of Your Subconscious Mind* by Joseph Murphy:

(Scan the QR code or hold down Ctrl and click the link)

http://www.amazon.com/The-Power-Your-Subconscious-Mind/dp/1434440826

and the second is, *Be the Change* by Ed & Deb Shapiro:

http://www.edanddebshapiro.com/be-the-change/

    I end up reading both within the next two days and they have some similarities. I like the concept of forgiveness in the sense that it's not about letting anyone off the hook for doing something bad, but about me letting go for my own good. I realise that Josh sending those DVDs and leaving the letter and introducing me to Clint has helped me at least actually start forgiving Steele. I know if he didn't do that, I would have probably had a lot more anger and sadness in me towards Steele and probably life in general.

    I am a little surprised by how the path he chose was exactly what I needed to get through. Clint's book choices for me definitely make me think about my thoughts and I have a greater knowledge about my thinking than ever before. On reflection I can see how my previous thought patterns would take me to a bad place in my own head, and knowing what I know from Clint, my thoughts would change my body chemistry and that body chemistry would actually work against me and drive those negative thoughts even further, commencing a vicious cycle. As I think of the time my first husband left me, I realise that when I finally came out of the spiral was when I changed my focus towards my ex rather than myself and this allowed me to change that brain chemistry, anger towards him was better than shame and self-pity towards myself. I guess one red brain response is better than two. It also meant that it still took me a long time to get over it.

    I feel a wave of sadness hit me when I start thinking about that time, not for my husband leaving, but because of my little Joshie taking care of me and never complaining even once. I suddenly feel again like I had let him down. I cry for my baby, but I acknowledge the thoughts and embrace the feeling of sadness because it is also laced with a feeling I can only describe as pride for my little boy pulling me through when I needed him most. Although I know I can't save him, I now have the steely resolve to do what he really wanted from me as his last wish, which was to not go down into the "Bad Place" again, and also to help others to not experience what he had.

    I cry and smile and laugh almost all at once. I'm beginning to understand myself a lot more. I am also analysing my thoughts and that awareness has made a massive difference. Yes, I still have feelings of letting Josh down, of being an inadequate mother and first wife, but I am getting used to not dwelling on it and just acknowledging the thoughts and letting it "pass" me by as the books suggest. I find those thoughts don't get me repeatedly thinking and rethinking them. I know I need to be specific about what I'm focusing on and right now it's supposed to be on grieving, but I'm actually feeling that I have actually done that over the last few days. I feel energised to want to do the work on preventing this happening to others. I call Rick and tell him my grieving period is over. I start thinking about what I can do to help this prevention process. I love the possibilities that pop in my mind and I am feeling very excited. I think Josh might be proud!

Chapter 24

Steele has been away from school for a couple of weeks now, nothing much has happened at school, but Taylor Harper has been quite talkative to me. I know she was a friend of Josh's and maybe my teary response at the funeral made her realise that his death affected me a lot as well. Emily (M1) has also changed a bit, I really think Josh's suicide has affected a lot of people. Everyone seems to be in a state of limbo I can't explain it, but it was like a lightning strike that has made a lot of us assess how our actions affect others. We have had some deep discussions amongst ourselves and even M1 was involved. I was surprised how many other students wanted to be involved.

We talked probably more deeply about things since Josh's funeral than ever before. I found our relationship went from being all about being popular to actually wanting to do something meaningful. His death had actually made a lot of people really think about themselves and the effect their behaviour was having on others. I know M1 was so worried that she had had an impact on Josh's death and when I told her about my DVD she actually cried, because she felt "released", because her guilt had really bothered her. I was then surprised by how supportive she was towards me. I felt comfortable enough to explain my history with Josh and why he would have sent me the DVD. She was like a different person after that, the whole group started talking and including others in the group and I can only say that it galvanised our whole year level. The shock of one of our own killing himself hit everyone hard. Having said that, none of us really knew what to do, how to help ourselves feel better and deal with it, until our principal advised us that Clint Adams was coming back to work with our group.

Chapter 25

I'm excited Clint is going to start taking Josh's year level through the start of his Full Mental Jacket Program, but at the same time he is going to take me and my teachers through his teachers' program, so that we can run things in the future and make the changes I know will be a little bit innovative and revolutionary. I can't contain my excitement when he walks into the lecture theatre with me and all my teachers and he starts to explain the Red Brain/Blue Brain training, which is all about making us aware of the brains conscious and unconscious responses and then also how the dialogue model works with that in mind.

While he is taking my group through this, I look around the group to see their responses and I can tell that this information and the manner in which he delivers it is hitting the mark. He is a naturally engaging man and you can feel his passion for his topic. Here is someone who is very passionate about this work and you feel a sense that as a school this is part of a much bigger experience. I can't explain it, but I have been to seminars and forums about education and change management and various programs, and I can honestly say this one makes the most sense, it's remarkably simple and yet remarkably inspiring. While I sit there and consider the implications, I realise how much I "missed" my dream, which was to make a difference and change my student's lives. I suddenly feel like this program can do what I always wanted even as a young teacher. I actually feel a tinge of guilt that none of us from the education sector had done this, but also feel excited that me asking the question has prompted Clint to design a program for students, when all he ever did was stuff for a workforce.

He takes us through the Blue Brain / Red Brain stuff and then explains the feedback component, where we all nominate three to five people on the faculty, including me, to give feedback on three things: Things they want you to start doing, things they want you stop doing and then things that they want you to continue doing. They also do their own where they predict what others will say about them. Clint explains that this is a technique her learnt from Leading Teams.

(Scan the QR code or hold down Ctrl and click the link)

http://www.leadingteams.net.au/

But he says that lots of people found it very confronting to say these things to people directly, so he changed it to be written down and given to him, and he then has a one on one with each person and goes through their feedback with them and develops an individual plan with that person based on their feedback. The self-forms gives him a heads up of whether they are self-aware of how they come across to others.

As much as I would like to think I'm a good principal, I also know there have been many times I have been too scared to confront senior staff on their performance, I also realise that my own fear of doing that has had an impact on the younger teachers, because their lives have been made more difficult because of my own inaction. I'm prepared to look at myself and wear the blame. I have coasted along and done an OK job, but if I was looking at myself now as I was when I started out, I would have been disappointed in myself. Having said that I am realistic in the fact that there are many schools and many years and none of them have done this work. I guess I just followed the rules and none of us thought outside of that. I also suspect that anyone with ideas different to the Education Department don't go any higher. It takes a kid's suicide and an outsider to come up with something out of left field. I can't help but think of a saying by Victor Hugo, 'Nothing is as powerful as an idea whose time has come.' The idea is here and its time has come and I can't wait. I LOVE my job again! I feel inspired and feel an energy inside, and I know I'm BACK!

Clint explains to my team how we can structure opportunities for new students, who have just started at the school, who are in a new group and to build positive routines into the curriculum. Things like, them analysing their own thoughts in a thoughts diary and also having "structured" and controlled conversations facilitated by the teachers, with the ultimate aim of making more robust individuals and also developing a student culture we actually want. It also promotes conversations students don't normally have, which in turn leads to better feedback in terms of behaviours others are not happy about. Again, I feel a little silly when I understand the simplicity of the program, but Clint has a way of making it seem simple. I still worry that the higher levels in the Education Department won't go for it, because it definitely challenges their thinking. There is a saying, 'That nothing stifles innovation like an expert.' Unfortunately, those at the top think they are experts because they have been around so long, but unfortunately, they do the same things over and over so it is going to be tough.

I know the young me wants to make changes, but the old me still worries that the people who determines my future don't think this way. I hate the fact that I don't stand up and SHOUT when that is exactly what I want to do. I have seen and heard Clint's Blue Brain/ Red Brain training and I know that I have sat on the top end of the dialogue model. I have been what Australians call a "soft cock" the one who is too gutless to do what they "know" is right. I reflect on that thought for a moment and ask myself some pretty big questions. I really know that Clint's program can change the way our students learn and develop to become better citizens, but I also know I'm one of the two or three who are in the running for higher roles within the department, and doing anything "radical" is not looked upon kindly from those who decide those roles.

I decide to go home and talk about it with my wife. She points out that I have been chasing these higher roles for the last ten years and I already know I have been close the last couple of times. She is the voice of logic, but I already know my answer and it is bundled up in a question. What is the right thing to do? The answer is: we have to run the Full Mental Jacket Program, the young me knows this can change lives and the old me wants to move up in the world. It is a desperate conversation I need to have with myself. I decide to let music be my guide. I'm a massive fan of Maroon 5 and I love their song *Daylight*, so while on the net I check out the film clip on YouTube. I hadn't seen the film clip so I didn't know there was some kind of competition where people sent in clips to go into the music video and this was the result. It's actually a little sad, hearing what some of these young people were saying. One girl talks about others at school as being the biggest bitches. Another person is hurting because her dad had died and she misses him every day.

Maroon 5 *Daylight:*

(Scan the QR code or hold down Ctrl and click the link)

http://www.youtube.com/watch?v=N17FXwRWEZs

While watching the clip, I can't help but think about my decision and this just confirmed that I'm here to help others and I just feel energised by the possibilities of the Full Mental Jacket Program. I know what I need to do and I'm pumped. So I'm singing loudly to the song.

The clip also made me realise how great it actually can be to be part of the human race. With all the negative things there is simply a lot of great humanitarians and love and goodwill out there. This is what I need to do more of. I'm determined to bring Clint's course to my school and also get promoted because I know it will change the game, but the key decision makers need to change their thinking and make things happen. I decide I want to be part of the change.

I listen to another song of theirs which helps me reflect on some people I lost on the way.

Maroon 5: *Memories.*

(Scan the QR code or hold down Ctrl and click the link)

https://www.youtube.com/watch?v=SlPhMPnQ58k

Chapter 26

Since Josh's funeral when I saw Emily crying uncontrollably, I have had to rethink what I originally thought of her. I had thought that because she was friends with the other Emily and also Steele, I had assumed she was like them. The more I thought about it, the more I realised she never really did anything nasty to Josh or anyone else for that matter. Her response at the funeral was more emotional than I expected and I thought I should speak to her to see if I was missing something. I saw her a couple of days later and decided to make contact and say hello. She was friendly back and I just thought I would talk about school because I didn't really know her and she didn't know me. The more we talked the more I started to like her. I actually realised that I didn't have any girlfriends. I was enjoying her company.

Over a few consecutive days we talked a bit, other Emily even came and spoke to me, it's like school had changed. Steele is nowhere to be seen. I heard he was getting some counselling because he was struggling to deal with being blamed for Josh's suicide. There are lots of other rumours too, but I don't get them from reliable sources, so I don't take them that seriously. I find that there is a calmness at school that wasn't there before, it's definitely the shock that this could happen. I think the basic human decency comes out in all of us and sometimes it takes an event, a shocking event that can make things change.

I still feel a lot of regret for not having done more to help Josh and save his life, but I also feel even more regret that I never made my feelings known to him. I know that will "haunt" me more, I will never know if he ever felt anything for me. I wonder if he was like me, too scared of possible rejection to make his feelings known and if he had, then maybe that might have changed his view on life. Thinking like this makes me sad, but I also have a determination to not let this get the better of me. I'm not enjoying life right now, but I can see the silver linings. I can see opportunities in the vibe at school, the interactions with Emily and even the other Emily makes me feel this is a time for some action. I'm not sure what action, but something needs to happen and I'm a little excited by that, as school for me has been a place to just lay low and not draw attention to myself. In a nutshell it was a place of "fear" for me and over time that takes a toll on how you feel and your perception of yourself.

I decide to play a Britney song that makes me think about Josh. The cry for him cleanses me a little and I actually feel better after I listen to it.

Britney Spears: *Everytime*:

(Scan the QR code or hold down Ctrl and click the link)

http://www.youtube.com/watch?v=8YzabSdk7ZA

    I love this film clip, clearly Britney Spears was a troubled person, I could see how being in the constant spotlight from a young age could make you go off the rails and lose a sense of reality. I can feel that vulnerability in the song and I don't want to think about what Josh was thinking about before he killed himself, but it does make me hope he had something that he could at least feel good about when his head was obviously swimming. I cry for him a little but then STRONGER Taylor comes to the fore.

    I saw Ellen DeGeneres here in Oz and she struck me as such an amazing person. Her visit highlighted some stories about her, in terms of the struggle she had, especially in coming out. I'm not gay but I can identify with struggling with things in life and I just love her attitude, her fun side and also the fact that Portia is from Geelong, where I actually grew up too. I feel I can identify. I find a couple of YouTube clips which just confirm what I think about them both. They really are inspirational in a time of adversity and I want to be like that. I really want to make a difference and I'm going to find a way, for Josh, BUT more for ME.

    Ellen DeGeneres' interview:

(Scan the QR code or hold down Ctrl and click the link)

http://www.youtube.com/watch?v=U-3S7jVBBG4

    Portia De Rossi's interview:

http://www.youtube.com/watch?v=-TrGNekDYpM&feature=endscreen&NR=1

    I especially liked this clip from New Zealand parliament about "Gay Marriage" and just think this politician is absolutely brilliant. I wish more had the guts to do this. It really is ridiculous when you hear his simple argument, that all they are doing is allowing for two people who love each other to have their love recognised in marriage. It's funny that we had to vote on this in Australia at immense costs to the country. At least sanity prevailed and they voted in favour of it.

(Scan the QR code or hold down Ctrl and click the link)

http://www.youtube.com/watch?feature=player_embedded&v=XCA8CA2hUoQ

Chapter 27

I catch up with Ben Gray to talk to him a bit more about what else we can bring to the program. I explain to him that we need to have a multi-layered approach:

1. We focus on educating his teachers on the foundation neuroscience/psychology, skills and behaviour and then helping them develop those in the youngest students, so that they build up good routines to develop those. I have taken his teachers through the overall process, but not this detail yet.

2. The older students need a different approach, so the teachers need to understand that. It's more of a "change" management approach, because they have already formed some habits and there may be strong relationships in place and already "set" groups. This involves taking the groups through a process of bringing up the "unwritten" rules that have developed and the associated behaviour that no one wants to talk about or deal with. Then specific facilitated conversations will take place to address these issues.

3. The parents are also educated on what they should be aware of. This is important on two fronts and that includes them knowing how to deal with their children whether they are the bully or the bullied. It also helps the parents, those whose children can be the aggressors and those who are a bit more defensive. There are so many "source" behaviours that stem back to our Fight or Flight reflexes, and this can became a very detrimental pattern of behaviours and thought patterns.

4. The next level is to focus on groups and help them proactively develop the type of culture they actually want as a group and then tease out what behaviour they want from each other. They also determine what their "rules" of engagement will be so there is less "fear" involved in having tough conversations, which is allowing younger students to get regular feedback from their peers about their behaviour. This gets them used to giving and receiving feedback, but with the skills to do it well.

Underpinning all this is the Red Brain / Blue Brain Training and specific "interaction routines". I show him a model I designed to help explain things better. The first is the C.U.P.E Square (see below). It basically represents a person and the components that ultimately affects behaviour and thought patterns. I change it to

CUBE Square, but the picture is PDF so I can't change it in time. The four components are:

- Conscious Thoughts
- Unconscious Thoughts
- Physical Component (Body)
- Emotions (Feeling)

They are all interlinked and as outlined in the Full Mental Jacket video's if we allow the Unconscious to be in charge, it leads where it leads and the body reacts accordingly and the emotions that come with it will continue. Over time we develop habitual automatic physical responses and think in those patterns as well. This is all fine until it becomes destructive for an individual. So the key is using the Conscious side to "Drive" the person, which is why the teachers need to set good routines for the new students, so they are guiding them to use the conscious side in a deliberate and healthy way, so that these become good habitual thinking and feelings.

C.U.P.E Square

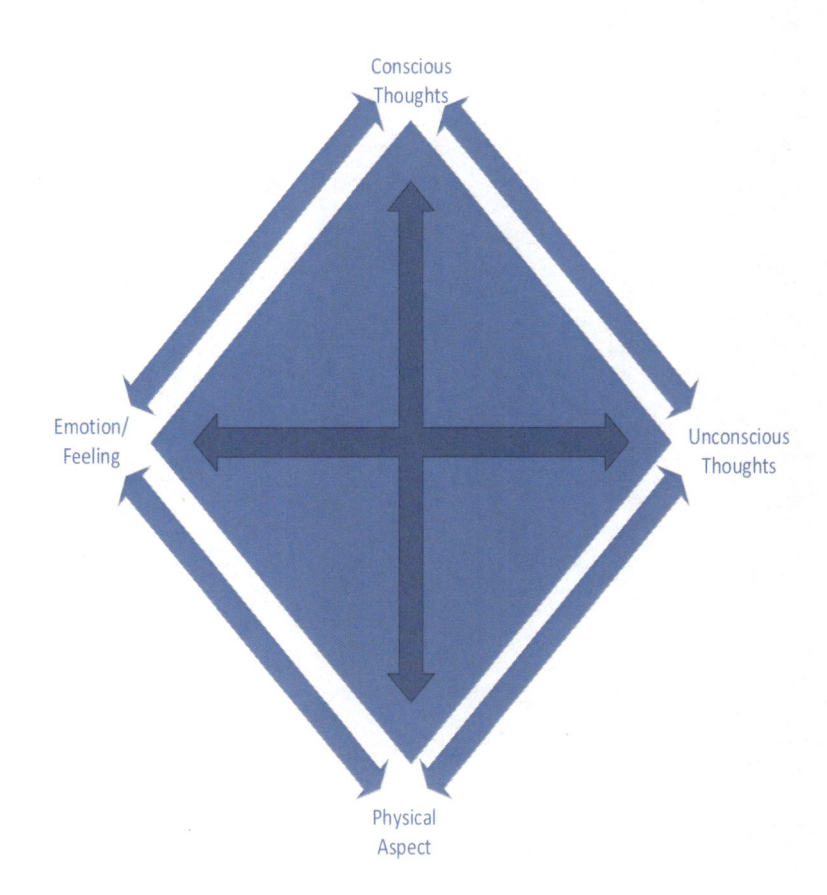

Conscious Thoughts

Emotion/Feeling

Unconscious Thoughts

Physical Aspect

I outline all the details to Ben, who is super enthusiastic about the process and the detail. He just says it is long time overdue and he then quotes Victor Hugo, 'Nothing is as powerful as an idea whose time has come.' We both agree that, it's time! This makes me think of the song, which is pretty cool.

It's Time: Imagine Dragons:

(Scan the QR code or hold down Ctrl and click the link)

http://www.youtube.com/watch?v=sENM2wA_FTg

We spend some time planning my schedule and the order in which I need to do things. I indicate to him that although this is the long-term plan, the shorter-term plan is to do some work with Josh's classmates and work through the process with them first. We leave each other with specific dates for me to catch up with his teachers first. The plan is then to start with Josh's class first and get to the rest of the school later. I hop in my car and play *It's Time*, the words are actually quite relevant and the song builds and is high energy. I almost want it to be our mantra through the process. *'It's time to begin isn't it?'* I'm a little excited that Ben is excited, because for a long period of time I had tried to get involved in a school's program dealing with bullying and harassment, but despite many attempts no one really showed much interest, no one in control of a school anyway. So the song is prophetic because **it is time.**

Chapter 28

The time begins and I finally get to start the process proper with Ben's teachers, I can tell that he is a good guy to work for, the teachers are generally happy. I have had experience with the Department Education in my previous role as an Injury Management Consultant and I know not all schools have great principals who have a happy team, but there is genuine excitement and what I have seen of Ben is genuinely good, he is a good guy, who just doesn't know how to progress his school. In comparison to other schools they get the job done, they are a good private school, but their performance has been relatively the same. What I love about Ben is that he wasn't happy with the status quo. No one was putting pressure on him to change anything, but he knew there was more and when he contacted me a while ago, he wasn't actually sure I could help him. He had seen a presentation I had done and he liked the concept of the psychological awareness and how it intersected with our interactions with others. He admitted he wasn't sure of the practicalities of it, but it intrigued him enough to make contact.

His call actually made me rethink my delivery, because I had thought I had made it quite easily understandable, so it prompted me to do some more research. I came across a great book, even though it compares marketing and management, it gave me significant information on why we are so different. It goes right into the psychology of left and right brain thinking. I had not really thought about this. I discovered I am very much in the extreme Right Brain group and I expect everyone to be the same, but we are definitely not.

(Scan the QR code or hold down Ctrl and click the link)

https://www.amazon.com/War-Boardroom-Right-Brain-Eye-Eye/dp/0061669199

I had to rethink my tact, which led me down a very different path, especially when I was trying to promote my program to industrial organisations. They want to see order and plans and steps, which goes against the Clint Adams grain. The Right Brain in me is about giving you great ideas and you should run with it, but this information made me realise that a lot of the people who end up in management roles are actually Left Brainers, so it is often a game of "selling" a "Right Brain" idea, to "Left Brain" decision makers.

I had to change my tact, I couldn't just go in with a great idea, they wanted to see plans, and rigour and all the things a Right Brainer hates, but I give a lot of credit to one of my managers Mark, who is an amazing man, I reckon he is either a suppressed Right Brainer or a Right Brainer worn down by the Lefties, but he is one of the most influential guys in my personal career. He definitely helped me, I say "helped" because he challenged my thinking, and caused me to think in terms of the opposite side. I now find myself, when designing change management initiatives, to take into account the other side of thinkers. If I didn't factor that in, I would be only catering to some of the group. The reality is we all think in a similar manner, but there are also consistent differences in the way we do that, so in order to have a good change management initiative, you need to factor this in. I have seen many programs, such as Lean or Six Sigma, which are supposed to get behavioural change, which they can do, but they tend to target the Left Brain, and leave out the rest, which is why they reach a "ceiling" and then the changes plateau out. I now really focus on those that don't think like me, but still feel comfortable in my knowledge that I need to do both, so it always involves working on good routines and rigour, which would have gone away from what I did in the past, but is what the Lefties like and understand, but then also focus on the behavioural, emotion and relationships of the individuals and the group as a whole.

Chapter 29

It's the morning of the first stage of the program, so I run through the Red Brain / Blue Brain session, which ends in them doing an activity identifying how you recognise someone in "Red Brain". Then we have discussions about what you can do to get someone out of Red and into Blue? It's always interesting to hear what strategies people use to do that. Most probably do things, and are effective, but they might not understand why it actually works. The type of answers I'm looking for is to ask the person a "high level" question, which effectively is one that requires the Prefrontal Cortex to help answer it. The reason this is important is that when you are in a "Fight or Flight" state, a lot of blood leaves the brain and is pumped to the limbs to quickly ready you for "danger". So asking the question requires the blood to be pumped back to the "Blue brain" because it needs that part of the brain to answer the question. This helps on two fronts, one it interrupts the Red Brain response and changes the physiological reactions, it also causes you to use the part of the brain, which is involved in coming up with solutions and this is the best part to be using when you want to come up with one. There is now more oxygen going into the brain and less going to your limbs to get ready for fighting or running.

I can tell that most of the teachers were responding well, they were laughing through the presentation. I always look at how they respond and they definitely understood the content and seemed to identify with it. After the activity, there are always lots of questions from the group, they can relate to their interactions at home, at work, people they know who show red brain patterns.

After the question time, I explain to them the process I use where they each need to give each other feedback. The format is simple as outlined previously, they write down the things they want that person to Stop doing, Start doing and then Continue doing. They do this in writing and send them to me and I do one-on-one debriefs with each of them to then work out a plan for each of them if required. I find those one on ones very insightful. I also know that with every group there are a lot of people who are "terrified" to give their work colleagues feedback, especially if it is negative for "Red Brain" reasons. It's either the person receiving the feedback gets angry or the person giving the feedback is too scared to give anyone negative feedback, so they usually put up with behaviour they don't like. In each case, the behaviour continues and then people hate their jobs, show passive aggressive behaviour themselves and often resent the workplace for not doing anything for them. I have seen this pattern in all kinds of workforces, education, police, health and various manufacturing organisations. So when I explain the process, I can see in the room that some are shocked, but I can also see some people look around the room at each other knowingly, as they are obviously going to be able to give someone feedback they haven't already. That always excites me.

I'm always amazed by what things people bring up. I had one manager get feedback from his entire team that he needed to stop digging in his ear when he was talking to them, because it drove them all crazy, because they couldn't focus on what he was saying to them at the time. Some say things like stop calling us "Country Pumpkins". Some have said stuff like, "Coming into my office saying, knock-knock just drives me mad." A lot of the results I see can come across as trivial, but it obviously is an issue for that person and they haven't dealt with it and now it turns out being something that has "grown" inside themselves and can be very disruptive in forming good relationships with that person. Many times when I have done mediation sessions with two people, it is these types of things that they allow to build up inside them and then suddenly the person has lashed out and we have a problem.

I explain the rules of feedback, yes there are rules, and you need to give feedback to help the other person improve. It's also important that the feedback is specific and focuses on the person's behaviour. Telling someone to stop being a tool is not helpful. The behaviour is the important thing. I always find this component interesting and can be very emotional for some people. We always see risk in telling someone something negative, because it can invoke negative reactions. Why don't most people say something to someone who pushes in line? The answer is we don't want them to react negatively and we really don't want anyone not to like us. In a lot of cultures, you are "taught" to be polite and be courteous and we have the view that everyone should be like that and when others are not, it does invoke strong emotional responses. It's funny when you think about "beliefs", they are learned and they have a massive impact, especially when someone has a belief different to ours, or appear to challenge ours, we tend to "dig" in. This can be good and bad. Regardless of what you believe in.

There is a need for people to actually understand how they "learn" their beliefs, because it is cultural, it can be determined by your nationality or religion and it is important for us to at least consider how it has developed. A lot of bad things happen because of opposing beliefs. People hate, people die, it's very powerful, but today is just about getting them to give each other feedback. I explain that they have a week to get their feedback sheets in to me, preferably by email.

I have a few come up and talk to me after the session saying that this is some of the most positive stuff they had seen. This type of talk always makes me feel heartened. I'm realistic that not everyone wants to get on board. I'm dealing with my own element now, adults, doing this with students is uncharted territory for me. I'm excited because I always wanted to help children and teens, but I just found it very difficult to have an effect on the policy makers and so I concentrated my energies on the general workforce, but this is a buzz for me, I'm genuinely excited.

Chapter 30

I have done my grieving; I know nothing will bring Josh back and I am working on myself to deal with that. I KNOW I'm not as emotional, I also have a task to fulfil, but I'm not using it to distract myself anymore. I have found the books Clint gave me, helped to really analyse my own thoughts and for the first time I have been very deliberate about that and it really has had a positive effect on me. I'm actually surprised how quickly I could actually deal with it. I catch myself feeling guilt about grieving so quickly, but this "catch" also reminds me that this is what Josh actually wanted. He did not want the self-pity I showed last time; he wanted a strong powerful mother who was going to help do what he wanted me to do. I am a little torn between both feelings, but the powerful one is on top this time, and that actually makes me feel great.

Rick and I are in a great space and he is so supportive and also very sad about Josh's death. I was surprised how hard it hit him, but I know he always wanted the best for Josh, and he also feels elements of failure. He was raised by a hard task master and felt he needed to go the same way with Josh as his stepdad, but that was probably not what Josh needed or responded to and he acknowledges he was probably very unproductive in his attempts and he feels an element of guilt. I give him the books that Clint gave me to read and talk him through the important parts. I know it helps him that I'm OK, so I know the books will help too.

I decide to play a song which is about seeing under the layers. Labrinth: *Beneath Your Beautiful*.

(Scan the QR code or hold down Ctrl and click the link)

https://www.youtube.com/watch?v=bqIxCtEveG8

I'm feeling so upbeat; things just can't happen quickly enough for me. Clint has advised that he will take the teachers through their things first, then the students and then all the parents. But I want to get involved, I feel energised. The waiting is going to be a problem for me and I ring Clint to see what else I could do.

It surprises me when he tells me that Steele had just rung him and felt the same way. He says he has advised Steele to read a copy of *You Are the Placebo* by Dr Joe Dispenza.

(Scan the QR code or hold down Ctrl and click the link)

https://www.amazon.com/You-Are-Placebo-Making-Matter/dp/1401944582

    Clint says it is one of the best books and it describes the power of the mind and how we are wired, how we operate and covers a number of the areas he will cover in his training.

    I'm intrigued and go get myself a copy from the bookstore after checking that they have it in stock. I start to read it immediately, I have this thirst for knowledge about myself, about humanity and how we interact and I do owe it to Josh and Clint. The books and the time spent with Clint has really changed my life. I am a very different person and I am open to wanting to know more so my interest in what he gave Steele, who is also on journey of his own I think could be helpful for both of us. When I think about it, he was never someone I would have ever interacted with if it was not for Josh's suicide. Sad but true!

    I also look him up on YouTube and there is an interview with him where he explains some of this and he talks about some of the neuroscience Clint says he bases some of his programs on. It does make you think a little differently about the way you think and the way you learn.

(Scan the QR code or hold down Ctrl and click the link)

https://www.youtube.com/results?search_query=joe+dispenza

Chapter 31

I am feeling anxious at home; I have been doing my "thoughts diary" as Clint suggested and I am a bit shocked by how many negative thoughts I have had. I start to notice them more and given the insight Clint has given me, I really do work on my "subconscious" in a conscious way, which would seem to make little sense, but the lesson I learnt is that the conscious is what the subconscious responds to and tries to work with. If you can get your conscious thoughts under control, it spills over into the subconscious and that can then work FOR you rather than against you, which is why things like affirmations can work for people. If you say it enough, it might sink into the subconscious and then you can believe it will happen. You really need to convince both your conscious and subconscious about something. If you "really" are not convinced about something, saying it won't do anything because your subconscious is really not convinced and it won't happen.

I love the fact that Clint didn't tell me what to do. He gave me information and let me go. I had lots of "Aha" moments along the way. I find myself really thinking about how I think. The books have taught me to think of my thoughts as things that "pop" into my head. In the past I might have kept letting it bounce around in my head, but realise now it is mostly memories of events that have occurred or what could happen, none of it is real anymore or maybe ever been real. If it's negative, I can consciously manipulate it or just let it slide by with some acknowledgement but nothing more. This realisation is very much something that I would say changed my life. I was in a very bad way whenever the thought that I had been responsible for Josh's death. I would really beat myself up and wish I hadn't done those things and try to think of things I could have done differently or done better. I recognise this was never a "thought battle" I could win, because he was dead and I was now focusing my thoughts on a memory or a future outcome that could never actually occur. I can never take back what I had done and I can never do other things to stop him dying. I can deal with the thought that I can do things to prevent this happening to others. I can change my view and change my behaviour, I'm actually thankful that I can do this and I got this great book from Clint called,

You Are the Placebo by Dr Joe Dispenza:

(Scan the QR code or hold down Ctrl and click the link)

https://www.amazon.com/You-Are-Placebo-Making-Matter/dp/1401944582

I start to think of ways that I can appeal to youth and others like me to make a difference and "rally" others. I talk with my parents and my sister Grace, and we all seem to be getting involved to do something positive. It's actually a very uplifting and defining moment for the Connors family, because we are doing it together and my parents are actually positive about being involved and they are brainstorming and giving suggestions to me and Grace. I just feel the positivity and it's the first time in many years that we have all been together to do that type of stuff. I have some great ideas in my head about how I can contribute going forward.

I'm a little nervous and excited because I am going back to school tomorrow and Clint is supposed to be running some group sessions with me and the other students in my year level. I start checking out some YouTube clips about inspirational people and I find this one which is pretty cool and it just shows how a mind shift and some perseverance can change your life.

Arthur: Guy and Yoga:

(Scan the QR code or hold down Ctrl and click the link)

http://www.youtube.com/watch?v=qX9FSZJu448

I then find this one on an inspirational two-legged dog. It's such an uplifting story. Amazing two-legged dog:

(Scan the QR code or hold down Ctrl and click the link)

http://www.youtube.com/watch?v=7f1ovurzU2s

Chapter 32

Well today's the day where I run the sessions with the students. I arrange to meet Steele in Ben's office, knowing he had not been at school for a while, so I knew he would be anxious. There would still be some students who would have some negative feelings towards him. I know he has come a long way, but this day is likely to be tough, given the time away. I have seen him "grow" and confront some of his demons. I have heard him take responsibility for his behaviour, but the others haven't seen that, so today he does need someone in his corner, without limiting what others need to get off their chest, even if that is scathing of what he did. The discussion will be facilitated by me and I'm confident I can keep it from getting out of hand, but I want to prepare Steele before he goes in, and discuss a strategy for the first session.

I meet with him and Ben, and his parents are there as well. I ask him what his plan is, to ascertain where his head is at. He says he is nervous but would like to address the group before the session. He says he wants to point out that he is sorry for his behaviour and that he is taking responsibility for his actions. He indicates he would like to tell them of Josh's wishes from the DVD he received and of his intentions to help with the changes required going forward. I am extremely pleased with this plan, because it addresses the elephant that would be in the room. It might not change everyone's view of him but at least it gives them insight in terms of where he fits in and his desire to make things better. We talk a little bit more and then it's time to go.

The students are all in the large lecture theatre along with their teachers and I walk in with Steele and Ben. Steele's parents elected not to go in, not sure if their presence might inhibit the dialogue required to reach a good result. Ben takes up his place at the front of the lecture theatre and Steele and I stand behind him. The room goes silent and you can see some of the students whispering amongst themselves. There is definitely an eerie silence, which is no surprise. I had told Steele to expect this reaction, possibly even some abuse. Ben opens proceedings indicating that we are all saddened by the death of Joshua, but Josh had sent some specific wishes himself to various parties including me and Steele. He says today is about giving anyone in the group an opportunity to talk about the effects it has had on them, and sharing stories of Josh and focusing on a better outcome for the group going forward.

Before we start that process, Steele has expressed that he would like to address the group before we start. Steele then steps forward and you can hear the already silent lecture theatre seem to become even more silent. All eyes are fixed on him. I can feel the fear in him, his Adam's apple is bobbing up and down before he even speaks. Then he takes a deep breath and starts, 'Firstly, I would like to apologise to all those people I have hurt through my actions. I have met with Josh's mother and I sincerely regret that my actions have contributed to the death of Josh and her loss of her son. I can't undo what I have done, but I can try to make things better.'

Fighting back tears he continued, 'You don't realise how sorry I am, I had no idea I was having this sort of impact on him and since finding out, I have really struggled with dealing with that responsibility.' He choked back tears but ploughed through, 'I received a DVD from Josh, giving me a chance to redeem myself, I intend to try to do that. I have been thinking a lot, reading a lot, thanks to Clint Adams' help and I know we need to make changes individually as well as doing things that focus on the group and how we interact. I give you all my commitment to do my best to do that. I know I can't ever change my past actions, but I can change my future ones. When Clint starts today's proceedings and asks for discussion, please don't hold back on comments about me or wanting to start discussions about me. I need to hear what people "really" think about me. It might be tough for me to take, but don't worry about hurting my feelings, I obviously had not worried about that in the past when it came to others, so I am expecting that, and I understand I need to improve, and I REALLY need you to tell me how it is. I can't express that enough; I just need you to tell me how it is. I know Taylor Harper will hit me between the eyes, she already hit me on the nose, which I obviously deserved, so please let's get everything out in the open.'

There are quite a few who laugh at the end comments, there was some applause, not a lot but some. I look at the groups faces and you can see a few nods and looking around the room with some faces showing approval for what he said. I personally feel quite proud of what he has done. I know there is still some skin in this game for him. There may well be a few who do hit him between the eyes, but I am impressed by his attitude. I know the books have helped and his parents support have been invaluable. What he doesn't know is I had a private meeting with both his parents to talk to them about what they could do to help him and be a support, and to their credit they did exactly that. In fact from what Steele said, he couldn't believe how great they were through the process. I personally think that his father was a controlling kind of personality. While good-intentioned parents always think they know what is best for their children and Steele's dad has always thought he knew best, but this incident has forced him to re-evaluate. Once they got past the fear of what could happen to their son from a legal point of view and then when Vicki met with them and laid out her intentions, which was to follow through with Josh's request, it allowed them to evaluate the incident and Steele's involvement with clearer heads. This is definitely more of an exception than the rule. If Vicki had been filled with anger and hatred towards Steele, this could have been a very different outcome. I should give a lot of that credit to Josh for leaving the letter he did for her, because it changed her focus, which in a funny way has helped my cause, as a large portion of my program is about directing your focus and helping your body and mind come along to where you eventually want it to go.

After Steele finishes his address, Ben reintroduces me to the group and I explain to them what is going to happen over the course of a few weeks, we will be running them through my Full Mental Jacket Program. I then explain what is going to happen today. I explain that I will take them all through the first section which is my Red Brain / Blue Brain training to give them all some insight into what is happening in their heads and bodies and how that affects their interactions with others and how it also frames up their own thinking, which again affects how they interact or in some cases inhibits interaction with others. I go on to explain where we will run what I call a "Fishbowl" conversation, where they will then have an opportunity to put any issues they have out on the table and have time to discuss them with anyone. I then run them through the training.

We have a break after the training and I talk to Steele and Ben because I know this "Fishbowl" part could also be very tough for Steele, as none of us know what the group is likely to say. They seemed OK when Steele addressed them earlier, but emotions can bring out anger and sadness and, in some cases, especially with bullying, SHAME. It makes me think of an article and books I read on Shame.

(Scan the QR code or hold down Ctrl and click the link)

http://www.breathwork.com.au/PDFfiles/AnatomyofShame.pdf

The thoughts about the article reminds me that it is important to have some of that Shame expressed today, rather than have these young people carrying it around and adding their own weight to themselves. A large part of this work I do is about getting individuals to understand themselves a little better, which should allow them to understand others a bit better, but then to do things in a proactive and constructive manner.

With Steele and Vicki, I only pointed them in directions to explore themselves, their thinking, their biology and "beliefs". Belief is an interesting word, they can also be called Mental Models, but whatever you call them, you need to be aware what they actually are. Beliefs can be very positive; they can also be very destructive. I'm not just talking about religion, which can be very positive and very negative. It is my view that Beliefs or Mental Models and Shame is very much intertwined, as the article touches on. What we "believe" about ourselves naturally comes from our experiences and our interactions. If we are constantly belittled from a young age and "shamed", we can believe we are stupid, or ugly or no good. When this happens, the results are more likely to be negative. The opposite is also true if you have a positive environment and are encouraged, you can have very positive self-belief. I start to think about a song which just pops in my head.

Ugly by Sugarbabes:

(Scan the QR code or hold down Ctrl and click the link)

http://www.youtube.com/watch?v=4nD2vZfdzGg

Chapter 33

I'm facing the group now, they have returned from their break and ordinarily I would ask if anyone has something to say and leave it to the group to decide, but I had a prepared plan and I call in my star, Vicki. I introduce her to the group, for those that didn't know her. This is Vicki, Josh's mum, she has something she would like to say to the group before we have some conversations.

Vicki starts by saying thank you to those who attended Josh's funeral and for the condolences she received from them and the school. She then goes on to explain what Josh had indicated in the letter he had left behind. She doesn't go into the detail of her previous breakdown but does touch on the fact that in the past she would have dealt with this situation differently. She explains to the group how she had met with Steele and his family and was not bitter or angry towards Steele, that she acknowledges he played a part in Josh's death, but then on many levels there were many contributors to it, including herself and Josh's stepfather. She goes on to say that nothing we can do can bring Josh back and undo what is done, but we can focus on a more positive future for this group of people and maybe even future students who will attend the school. She finishes by saying that bullying is a social problem and we are all part of the problem and need to all be part of the solution, and she and Steele have made a commitment to be part of that solution. She walks off to applause from the crowd. I am quite proud of her and follow her and tell her that, and also that Josh would have been proud of her too.

I then turn to the group and start the session. I explain the rules of this feedback or fishbowl session to them. I want someone to start this off strong, experience in these sessions has taught me that if you have someone you know will not be defensive and can get the conversation started, then it creates a "safer" passage for others to get more involved. It is the crucial part of these sessions and knowing that Steele already mentioned Taylor Harper, I decide to open with her and ask her a question directly. First, I ask her to stand up, which she does. I hadn't met her so wasn't really sure what to expect, I knew she had bopped Steele on the nose in class, which made me think she might be a tough young lady, but I'm surprised to see quite a light-framed young lady with a pretty and friendly face. I do notice from her body language that she is a little uncomfortable and has tried to make herself look even smaller by the way she holds herself and the way she is holding her hands, but she is up.

I look directly at her and ask her how she feels about this process? She replies that she thinks it is a good idea as she knows a lot of people have been waiting for some kind of intervention, because there is tension and still an element of shock within the school. She goes further to say that it has been good without Steele being at school and it has allowed people to talk amongst themselves. She turns to Steele and tells him, 'Don't get me wrong, Steele, I heard what you said and what Josh's mum said and I also want us to move forward, but if you had been here it would have been more difficult and we needed this type of session before you were allowed back. I thank the school for doing it this way. I do miss Josh; he was my friend and obviously I was extremely angry at you when I decided to punch you. I had seen you do lots of horrible things to him over the years and to be brutally honest with you, I don't think you are a very nice person and although you say you want to do the right thing going forward, I say the proof will be in the pudding as they say. If you can turn your behaviour around, that would be great, but unlike Josh's mum I still have a lot of anger towards you and towards many others including myself. I am especially angry that certain teachers and students have seen you do horrible things to Josh and others and no one did anything, other than laugh. I know a lot of people were scared you would turn on them if they said anything, but surely teachers and some of the tougher students could have done something. A lot of my anger goes to them as well as you Steele.' But I also realise I was one of those students who was scared you would turn on them, so I also did nothing, but I have done a lot of thinking since he died and I need to be stronger within myself, because I didn't really like who I was.

When Taylor sits down, I can tell on her face it was hard on her, it's not easy to confront people, especially when it could mean long-term ramifications for you and when you have seen these same people have devastating effects on others close to you. I am the facilitator of this and I decide I want Steele to respond. I don't know his reaction, but it was exactly what I wanted from Taylor, because what she said, might be exactly what others are thinking but were too afraid to say and by her going first, it might just mean others will open up and talk about this. What she said was actually very brave and she didn't spare the teachers involvement either. I thank her for her honesty and point out that I agree that there are a number of actions and also inactions which has led to this point.

I ask Steele if he would like to respond, and when I look at him, I notice he is crying, but to his credit he stands up and thanks Taylor for her honesty and again acknowledges and agrees with her assessment of events. He goes further to say that nothing he can ever do will bring Josh back or change what he has done and he can never hide from that involvement, but he can again commit to making things better. He wipes tears away the whole time, and then stops and looks Taylor dead in the eye and says, 'I promise you Taylor that the old me is gone and if you or anyone else even sees glimpses of the old me, you have my permission to punch me in the face!' He sits down to a silent crowd, they are obviously in shock, probably because Taylor "went there" and he didn't respond the way they thought he would. WOW! What a great start!

I address the group by saying, 'Can we please acknowledge the bravery that Taylor just showed, and I'm so impressed by that because until we raise the issues, we won't address the issues, thank you Taylor.' The group clap loudly and I feel a sense of relief and also a feeling of optimism that we might actually get somewhere today. I then also ask them to acknowledge how Steele has responded and the commitment he has made. Again, there is applause for him as well.

When I ask who would like to say something, and I'm a little surprised when one of the teachers actually stands up and says he agrees that he and other teachers have seen some poor behaviour from students towards other students, and seem like they do nothing, but he points out how frustrating it is for them when they have intervened in the past and the "punishment" for these students are not effective, they don't care about doing yard duty or detention and often if they are suspended the parents make complaints about the teachers. They then get investigated and in many instances, they feel like the investigator doesn't believe them and more often than not they come to some kind of "deal" where they agree to drop the complaint and have the punishment either reduced or completely quashed. Over time it's just easier and less pain in it for the teacher to not get involved. We get little support from the higher levels. The teacher turns to Ben and says, *'Ben, you know all this, our education department and board members don't support us enough, I know they put pressure on you as our principal, but I think we need to start putting pressure on them to come up with some reforms. The education system is based on such an old model, and it continues to breed relationship issues and students feeling less than valued if they don't perform well in this system. Grades seems to be the only real KPI that anyone looks at, not whether we have great future citizens and people coming out the other side.'*

As he is talking, it reminds me of an article on the net I read only recently, while trying to work out how I can be more effective to the school.

Time for an Education System Makeover:

(Scan the QR code or hold down Ctrl and click the link)

http://www.forbes.com/sites/work-in-progress/2013/03/05/time-for-an-education-system-makeover/

The teacher continues outlining that to move forward we need to change the way things are done, but need to address not only the support of the Education Department and Board, but involve the parents somehow. This idea intrigues me and I start to think of what we can do to apply it. It's also interesting what he is saying about why the teachers "don't" often intervene. I can see when I apply a "Change Management Model" I read about, that identifies what they term "Vital Behaviour" you can see it's the system, it's the parents and teachers all involved and to change it you need to address those vital behaviours. The model comes from a book:

(Scan the QR code or hold down Ctrl and click the link)

http://sourcesofinsight.com/influencer-the-power-to-change-anything/

The model basically says to change anything you need to address a minimum of four of six areas. The model has three categories to work on and each of those contains two components making the six. So, in a nutshell, you need to work on changing each individual's behaviour, the group and what they do to help individuals make the change and also the environment, which in this case involves the system and parents as well.

After the teacher finishes what he says, Ben stands up and thanks the teacher for his contribution. Ben also says he acknowledges his own involvement in this, and that he too has felt that pressure from the parents and also the department and board, and he agrees that things need to change and he is committing to help make that happen. He says to the group that he will setup some brainstorming sessions with the faculty first to see what they can do to work on what they need from the Education Department.

I ask the group if anyone would like to go next and a female student puts her had up and I ask her what she has to say, and she identifies herself as Emily, she indicates that she had known Josh for a very long time when his and her parents were friends, and he was actually her friend when she was younger. She says she feels ashamed of herself for ignoring him in high school, she says she was scared that it would have meant social suicide for her if others knew that she had been friends with him, so she deliberately chose not to acknowledge him at all. She indicated that she did feel bad for him when Steele would pick on him, but didn't feel she could stick up for him or say anything or it would be her on the outer. She starts to cry a little and says that she wishes she had been able to be more courageous and stand up for not only an old friend, but for another human being who was in distress. She says she heard what Steele and the other teacher had said and she agrees that moving forward they need to come up with some kind of intervention to work on a strategy to change the school environment, one which is sustainable for future students. She stops and tells everyone about Josh's message to her and she starts to cry again. She says she wants to be part of the solution. She wants to make things right! When she is done, there is roaring applause. I stand up and thank her for doing this.

A few more stand up and point out how much they dislike the bullying, how it affected them either directly when they were points of exclusion or were made to feel bad because they weren't wearing the right clothes or look as good as others or weren't as skinny or athletic or smart. The list of things went on, but each time they spoke, you could feel the pain they were feeling, a lot cried, a lot you could see felt angry, they had pent up anger that had been there for a while, but had been held in.

I was surprised how many wanted to get this off their chests but one other that stood out was from another student who was also named Emily. She stood up and said, I would like to apologise to a lot of you for being such a bitch. I have done and said nasty things to you and also talked negatively about a lot of you. Like the other Emily I also have used my social status as a mask, I don't feel good about doing those things and since Josh died, I have been really thinking about what I have done. What I have seen and also what I should have done. I have encouraged students like Steele by laughing at others and I can see that it was people like me who stopped Emily from acknowledging that she had been friends with Josh, because, while I'm being honest, I probably would have ridiculed her for it and that probably would have meant she wouldn't have done that again. Listening to everyone here today has helped me understand how we affect others and Joshua's death has hit me harder than I thought because he was one of us. I really didn't know much about him, I know I made lots of assumptions about him and his clothing choice and stuff like that but now he is gone and I think about my role in that. I had no idea that other Emily had been friends with him and I feel awful that she felt like she could not share that with me and I understand why.

I'm so blown away by what this group had shared and some of the really "crunchy" issues they raised. Having only ever done this with adults in the workplace, I really was not sure of how this would go. I felt that they were even more courageous than a lot of adults I had done this with before. I decide we should end today's session here and again thank everyone for their participation. I advise them we will be running another session first thing the next day, but tomorrow is what I call a "destination setting day". I inform them this upcoming session is focusing on the future not looking at the past.

I watch the students stroll out and both Steele and Ben stay behind. I tell them that the day went really well. I can tell from their expressions that they also thought so, but I can tell it has also been taxing on them, especially Steele. I have done this a few times and know it is a combination of the things said in the session today and also the build-up and expectations of what might happen in the session that takes its toll at the end of the session. I tell them to go home and rest and I know they will sleep well. They both agree and leave the lecture theatre.

As I am packing up some of my equipment, one of the students who spoke up today, the first Emily comes in to talk to me. She was the one who had known Josh when she was much younger and was emotional today and brave in what she said. She tells me she needs my help, that since she has received the message from Josh, she has been feeling more and more depressed because of her behaviour or as she points out lack of action. She says the fact that Josh identified her and pointed out one of the songs he identified her behaviour with, has kept her thinking that she was responsible for his death. She says she had heard that I may be able to help her because she feels she is about to blow up. She tells me this has really hit her hard and the things she said today had been waiting to come out and she had been repeatedly thinking about what she had witnessed and done nothing about. She had been thinking about her behaviour including when she had laughed at Josh and the things, she had told her friends and not told them about Josh.

I tell her I am happy to try and help her. The first thing I talk to her about is the events and how she has reacted to them the first time they actually happened. She tells me when she first read the letter and watched the song's film clip, she just had such a pang of guilt.

I ask her what that "felt" like, she looks at me a little shocked and says, 'Well, I felt this feeling of "pain" is the best way to describe it!'

'I felt a surge in my stomach and then I just felt like crap.' I ask her about what she was thinking at the time. She tells me she just felt guilt and a touch of shame that she did nothing when he needed her, she also said she felt weak that she hadn't had the courage to stand up for her own views and said anything. I ask her how she feels when she thinks about that event. She seems surprised and says, 'I already told you how I felt when it happened.'

I reply, 'That's not what I asked, I asked how do you feel when you think about the event now, not how did you feel about it when it happened, which was what you answered?'

She says, 'Well, I felt the same, why would it be any different?'

I explain, 'Well, the first time it happened you were responding to a very real stimulus, but now you are responding to your memory or thoughts of an event that has already been and gone. Do you see the difference? Your thoughts are bringing a repeated response.'

She looks at me and I can see her face shows an element of surprise but also intrigue and she slowly says, 'Oookaaay, why is that significant?'

I tell her, 'Well, at the moment when you think of the memory of that event, it starts a chain reaction of events in your body, the same as it did the time you actually experienced it, but it's now not a "physical event", it's a psychological one that you now generate from your memory. Your own thoughts now make you relive the event and now experience the same reactions as if it was happening again. While the brain reacts slightly differently to a memory than a real event, it still has an effect and if it is a highly emotional memory that you keep replaying, it can have a negative effect on you depending on how long you focus on it and what kind of reaction it brings out.'

I explain to her that she can't ignore what has happened and even change what has happened but she can use this memory in a different way to move forward, rather than dragging her backwards. I tell her to also keep a "thoughts" diary, like I did with Steele. I give her the same instructions I gave him, which was to track what thoughts pop in her head for 1 week and then at the end of each day she should check the list and mark which are positive and which are negative thoughts. She agrees to meet with me in a week's time and we can go through the results.

It's been a long day and while I'm excited by the progress we made today, I'm also quite tired, facilitation of this kind is quite taxing, as you have to concentrate the whole time, constantly scanning the room, analysing whether what the others are saying could ignite arguments or even violence. I also have to scan to see if someone is affected by what is being said but are just quiet and internalising things. I have a lot of responsibility running these, because if someone hears something that could drive them to self-harm or harm others and I have encouraged them to say it, I need to be able to work with the affected person to frame what is said differently, and so they don't go down that path. I'm in my car heading home feeling a bit drained but also excited by where the discussions went today. I decide to play one of my old favourite songs, which was also the first song I heard when I migrated with my family to Australia in 1984.

Flame Trees: Cold Chisel

(Scan the QR code or hold down Ctrl and click the link)

http://www.youtube.com/watch?v=K8KgP2aOXcA

Chapter 34

After the session at school, I decide to stay back and talk to Clint. I'm not sure why exactly but I feel some relief for actually saying what I said today, but still feel kind of hollow, because of what Josh thought of me before he died. I replay the words of the letter in my head and also the song.
Caught in the Crowd:

(Scan the QR code or hold down Ctrl and click the link)

http://www.youtube.com/watch?v=GIDarYJHCpA

Sadly the lyrics are exactly how I feel, I wish I could go back and do it again, because I would be someone, he could call friend and I am sorry. I'm not sure why, but I feel that Clint can help me deal with this guilt. I know he has been working with Steele and I was pleasantly surprised by Steele saying what he did and taking accountability for his own actions.

After everyone has left and he is packing up, I approach him and tell him how this has affected me, he asks me some questions about how I felt when it happened and then how I feel when I now think about the event. At first, I didn't really understand why that would be important, but I have had some time to really think about things, I can see why it actually is very important. Clint explained the first as the actual event, and me thinking about the event after that as the memory of that event. The first is a "physical" stimulus and the second is now a psychological one. The bit about this that I think is significant for me is that the first event was getting the letter, reading the letter and seeing the songs film clip and this generated some high emotions for me. The "events" afterwards is me thinking back to these things, and that is significant for me, because I think in the first instance I had no control over how the first event affected me, but now I have control, or at least could have control of how I use those memories and this is a very positive step for me.

Clint also asked me to keep a diary of my thoughts and after three days, I realise how hard that is to actually do. I'm also surprised by how many thoughts actually pop into my head during the day, sometimes they are just random things, sometimes I am actively thinking about things. I find Josh's letter pops into my head a few times and I still get the associated "wave" of guilt and feelings in my stomach, which are still unpleasant. I "catch" myself now because of the thoughts diary, and try to consciously think about that thought, what it means, how it makes me feel and what

I can do to make it less unpleasant. I find myself self-talking a lot as I try to figure out what I can do to help myself. I find that as I analyse the thoughts, even though the unpleasantness is still there, it doesn't seem to last as along, because I am now consciously thinking that this is just a thought and a memory, so I can deal with it because that's all it is.

I start checking out the net for ideas on changing thoughts and find these. Ten tips to overcome negative thoughts:

(Scan the QR code or hold down Ctrl and click the link)

http://tinybuddha.com/blog/10-tips-to-overcome-negative-thoughts-positive-thinking-made-easy/

Eight tips to change negative thinking:

http://socialanxietydisorder.about.com/od/selfhelpforsad/tp/8-Tips-To-Change-Negative-Thinking.htm

I find each of these quite helpful, especially the last one, which actually gives you information on a 'thoughts' diary. I also like the view that you don't want to stop the thoughts, but you want to make it "float" by. This idea about mindfulness also intrigues me, because the more I think about it, the more I realise I tend to daydream and not really be present in the "now" a lot of the time. The other tips I also find useful and decide I want to try some of these things, like yoga and meditation. I also think that I do need to be more assertive, because I am a person who probably runs from conflict. I want people to like me and I don't deal well with criticism. If someone was to say something negative about me, I would get sad and probably cry. I want to change this part of me. The other tip I like is to do something for someone else. I'm not sure what yet, but I will think about it. Finally the other tip was to surround yourself with positive people. I think about the last two tips and an idea pops in there, surely Steele could do with someone to at least support him, I think I could help him and at the same time he could help me.

I also think of Taylor Harper and also M1 and what they both said and how it has affected them. I start throwing ideas in my head of what I could do to co-ordinate things and help these guys all get on the same page with some solutions, which ultimately is aimed at doing what Josh wanted, which was to stop this from happening to others in the future. I'm not sure exactly what I can do, but I think I should do some brainstorming with these guys to begin with. I decide to call Clint as I have his card to see if he has some thoughts.

I tell him about what I have found on the net and that I feel energised to want to do something, even though I'm not sure what. He says I need to start with the end in mind. He asks, 'What exactly do you want to see at the end of whatever you want to do?'

I say, 'I guess I want for all the students at this school to be able to get along and not have anyone judging others and doing nasty things to one another, like fighting and talking behind others backs. I just want there to be positive relationships between them and have an environment where students genuinely look after each other and there is a feeling of community. I guess it's a little bit idealistic and maybe it's a pipedream, but I think regardless we can improve on what happens now.'

Clint asks, 'OK, let's think about what is causing what we get now?'

I say, 'Well, some of the students' parents probably don't teach their kids how to treat people well, some people are selfish and only look out for themselves, this is probably learned at home. Maybe there is also no consequences for bad behaviour, here and at home. I guess sometimes people are too scared to make it known so the teachers probably can only act on what they see or hear about. Sometimes the teachers see it and do nothing about it. Sometimes we students see it and do nothing about it. I don't know there are a lot of variables here.'

Clint asks, 'Why do you think someone like Steele did these nasty things to others like Josh?'

I think about that before I answer, as I'm not really sure. I say, 'Well, some of the things he did was funny and he got laughs from others, which I guess encourages more of the same to get a "good" reaction to boost his ego I suppose, or makes him feel like he is popular and somehow admired by others, for being entertaining and funny. I suppose it could also be his upbringing, his parents may somehow bully him and he feels it's OK to then do things to others. I hadn't ever thought that maybe he could have been bullied by other students in previous years. I didn't go to primary school with him so don't know that history, but I know he is very competitive and his sister is really good at sport as well, so I think there is an element of that which might come from the family.'

We talk a bit more and discuss some options. I suggest I would like to organise a meeting after the next session we have scheduled at school with Clint and ask for those who would like to be involved as a smaller group to brainstorm some options. I tell Clint, I like the questions he asked of me just then and would like to use a similar approach with the group so we can look at what we need to change, what is keeping this pattern of behaviour going. I hang up and feel quite good about things. I then call M1 and discuss this with her, she says she would be happy to be involved. I call Taylor who says she is happy to be involved too, but has some reservations if Steele and M1 are involved, because she says, actions speak louder than words, and while Steele seemed to be saying the right things, he hasn't really been back at school for anyone to see any change in his behaviour.

Chapter 35

Well, it's the second session with the group and I am feeling good knowing that Clint has indicated he will help me to be involved in a "movement" at the school and I am co-ordinating a group to do that. He indicates that the fact that we only had the first session and I am thinking this way is positive on two fronts. One, he says is, I am focusing on something other than negative aspects of the situation and two, I am looking to come up with a solution to a problem, if I was able to get enough people involved and can address the root causes of this, then some really good progress can be made.

We are back in the lecture theatre and he is running the session, Ben Gray and the others are all in the audience today. After a greeting he runs the whole group through the Red Brain / Blue Brain session and he also shows them his Blue Red Interaction Model and also the Blue Red Internal Cycle which he says he had been working on.

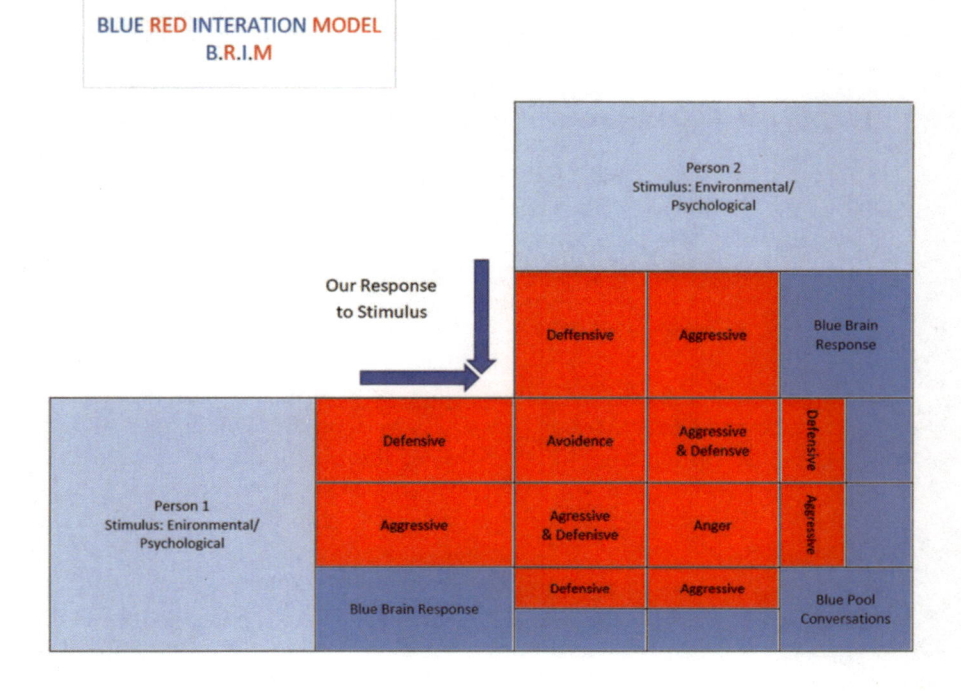

BLUE RED INTERATION MODEL
B.R.I.M

		Person 2 Stimulus: Environmental/ Psychological			
	Our Response to Stimulus	Deffensive	Aggressive		Blue Brain Response
		Defensive	Avoidence	Aggressive & Defensve	Defensive
Person 1 Stimulus: Enironmental/ Psychological		Aggressive	Agressive & Defenisve	Anger	Aggressive
		Blue Brain Response	Defensive	Aggressive	Blue Pool Conversations

He explains that if both individuals are defensive or aggressive (Red Brain) during a conversation or interaction, then it is more likely to end up in a red or negative response, either both become aggressive, or one does while the other backs away or both avoid dealing with the issue. In each case, they cannot have the conversation they need to deal with the issue in the best way.

For that to happen both really need to be in a Blue Brain frame of mind and this means they need to create the "safety" outlined in the Dialogue Model.

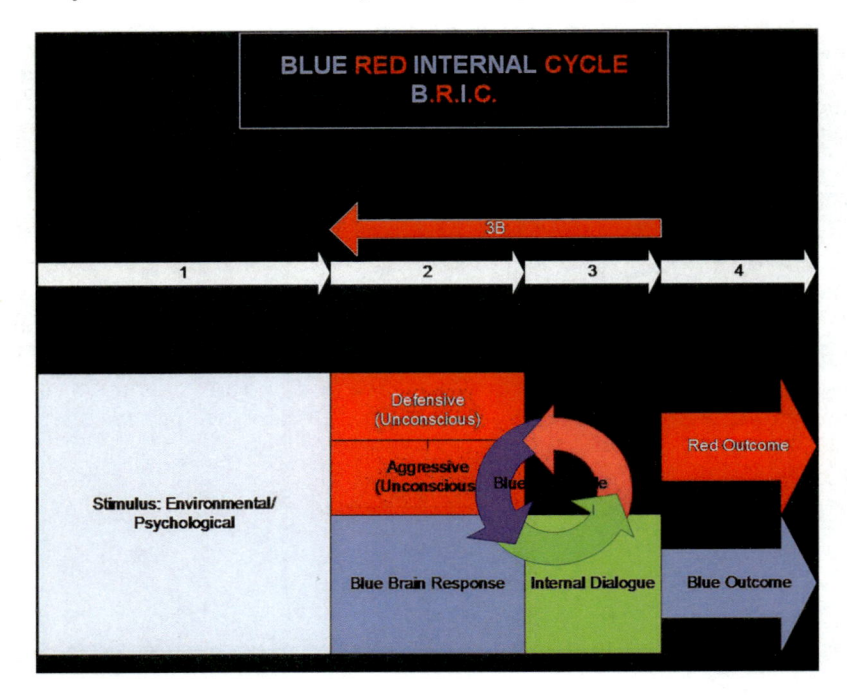

BLUE RED INTERNAL CYCLE B.R.I.C.

- Stimulus: Environmental/ Psychological
- Defensive (Unconscious)
- Aggressive (Unconscious)
- Blue Brain Response
- Internal Dialogue
- Red Outcome
- Blue Outcome

He explains that the second Model is the simplified sequence of events from a Stimulus to our "automatic" Response and then the Internal Dialogue we have ultimately determines what type of outcome we have.

He explains to us that the purpose of doing this session is to explain how fear and anger both prevent better conversations from happening and while someone in the conversation is angry or afraid, we will be less likely to come up with a good outcome.

He goes on to explain that he will be asking us to write down feedback for our classmates, to help them improve, in terms of behaviour we want them to stop, start or continue doing. He explains the rules of feedback and also advises that these sheets will come to him and he will catch up with individual students and give them their feedback. We won't know who it specifically came from other than it came from our classmates.

The session seems to go quite well and he ends it by explaining that I would like to say a few words. I go up and say that I had been thinking since the last session about how I could do something to help change the school culture and prevent this kind of behaviour from happening again. I go on to say I am not sure how to go about it, but would like to brainstorm with a group, who might be interested in joining me and setting up a sort of project team to see what they can come up with. I say that I would want people who have a genuine interest in doing this, I say we want those who have been bullied and those who have been the bullies, as well as input from teachers. I tell them the reason we want both (bullied and bullies) is that there may be things that only the bully can help with, because we are going to the behaviours and the motivations of those people to do some of the things they do.

I then ask that anyone interested please stay back and I can get their details if we didn't have it already. Taylor Harper, M1 and Steele all stay back, but there are a few others who also stay back. They are James Ward, who is a quiet guy who is quite a large guy and I suspect he gets teased a fair bit about his size. I suspect he may also be gay, but I'm not sure. Another is a Chris Davis, who is a good friend of Steele's and there is another girl Meg Reynolds who is a very shy person, very smart but not very social and I suspect a lot would call her a nerd. Lastly, Andrew Holtz who is quite small in stature and wears glasses and usually keeps to himself quite a lot, like Meg, I could see how he too would have been a target for bullies.

I have had a few discussions with Clint about how to take charge of this group, not really knowing if anyone would stay back, but I did have verbal confirmation from M1, Steele and Taylor, the extra four are a surprise. I take Clint's lead and outline that I have asked for this group to be formed with the sole intention of looking at ways we can make our school environment a safe one where all students look out for each other and help each other to become good "citizens" and we get the best education we can. I say, '*I know it's idealistic, but we haven't really put our minds to how we can do things better. Let's agree to meet tomorrow after school for two hours, I will get pizza delivered and we can go through ideas. I want you each to think about what you think has caused our current school environment to be what it is, list everything you can think of in terms of parents' bullies, timid students and teachers. Then think about ways we could address those "causes".*'

The group agrees to meet and do their homework before the session. We all disperse and go home. I'm feeling very good as I start to walk home and I'm a little surprised when Meg catches up with me and asks if she can talk to me. She goes on to say that she decided to join the group because as much as no one actively picks on her to her face she knows that people call her "Brainiac" and geek and similar kinds of things, but that isn't what bothers her. She says she just feels isolated and immerses herself in her school work, but doesn't really have any friends and no one tends to hang out with her. She starts to cry and I try to console her. She says I'm not sure I can talk about this in front of the group, it's not bullying but exclusion and I feel just as bad about it. She has thought about killing herself because she doesn't enjoy her life. This group is an opportunity for her and she just wanted to say thank you for saying what I did the other day and then suggesting this group. I had been thinking about what I could do for myself, and this just jumped out at me to be involved in. I have been reading lots of stuff on psychology and change, that I think could help the group going forward. Thanks Emily I just thought it was worth you knowing why I'm here, because I'm probably a surprise. I thank her for sharing with me and that I had no idea this was happening or at least that it was having this effect on her. We then go our separate ways.

Chapter 36

Next day after school, we all meet up as agreed. I start off by saying, 'Well, you heard why I wanted to form this group, but I think it might help if we went around the table to explain why you guys are here and what you want out of this. Steele, do you want to go first?' Steele says that we all heard what he had to say in front of the bigger group in Clint's first session, but he says since then he had really focused on what he could do. Josh was clear that he wanted to stop this happening to others, Steele thought about how "bullying" can be less destructive. He suggests we can focus on stopping the bullies, like him and/or we can help make individuals able to deal with things and make them more robust. To use a war analogy, we minimise the amount of people shooting bullets at others and at the same time we focus on giving the others better armour, minimising the risks of a fatal hit. Doing both would lead to a better result overall.

Steele continues, for himself personally he is here because he wants to atone for his behaviour, unfortunately someone had to die before his eyes were wide open. Before spending some individual sessions with Clint, he was starting to spiral downward in his own head. He could see how easily it can happen. He only experienced some exclusion from the other students when he came back and, of course, Taylor's kung Fu skills on his nose didn't help his mood. If anything, he started wanting to be punished, so he could say OK, I've had my whack, now let's move on, but with this situation he couldn't do that. Maybe time will do that, but he is here to try and make things right, so he can look at himself again without feeling guilt. That's it from him.

'Emily (1) what about you?' I ask.

She says, 'Well, when I heard you, Steele and Taylor say your bits in Clint's session, I felt I needed to be involved. When I found out about Josh, I was shocked, but started to ask myself if I contributed to what happened and when I heard what you said Emily (2), I knew like you, I did nothing to stop it and I also contributed to stopping you from doing something too. I realise if I had been less judgemental, you would have felt more comfortable talking about this with me and others. I may have reacted differently to Josh and you being friends with Josh. It's made me ask some questions about myself as a friend and a person really worthy of being someone others look up to, not just for looks and superficial things, but for something more. I may look like this confident person who has it all going on, but I freak out about a zit, because I seem to find it so important that others think good things about me. I have always had it drummed in to me at home to look good and work out and be thin, so guys will like me and I can be popular and life will be easier. But I'm in fear the whole time, that people will work me out, or when school ends, I have no one who really wants me in their lives. I worry about what others think about me, so religiously to the point that I don't want people to think I'm a dork so I don't try with my school work, because others equate being good at school work with being somehow unsavoury. I don't know how that happens, but it is an issue I would like us to think about addressing, because a lot of smart students 'act' dumb to fit in, when we should be all encouraging everyone to do well and still look good. That's it for me so far.'

'OK, Chris, what about you?'

'Well, I know like Steele I have also done things to Josh and others that I'm not very proud of. When I heard you guys all speak up, especially you Steele, I also started asking myself what I might have done to contribute to what Josh did. I looked on my own involvement and when I think about it, I would go along with things to get approval from others. The first time I did it, I really felt uncomfortable, but then as time went on things seemed to get easier. I started not having a conscience, like these kids deserved it or something and they didn't really resist and no one was saying don't do it. If anything, people were laughing about it and coming up later saying that prank was genius or something like that. It wasn't until Josh died that I stopped and went holy crap this is not good, I'm part of this and when Steele told me about the DVD, I was shocked, that it got to that and I was so in a different place that I never considered anyone else. I have just been feeling like crap with thoughts of Josh hanging from his roof going through my head and I really don't know how to get that thought out of my head. I ultimately want that thought out of my head and also change the way we do things here, so it can't happen to anyone else, and when I mean anyone else, I don't just mean Josh. I think about his parents, his relatives, people like Taylor who were his friends and really all those at school affected by this. I was actually surprised how people reacted at school. This school will never be the same, I actually think more people think behaviour like ours has been a bad thing, but were never prepared to say anything. Since seeing Clint's presentation I can understand that more, I have some ideas to share going forward, but that's my bit.'

'What about you, Taylor?'

'Well, you already heard my views on some of this the other day, but although I was reluctant to be involved initially, I am here to see our school change. I have seen too many kids being bullied, not just by Steele and Chris, and I have been part of the bullied and know others who have struggled and felt bad about themselves because of what others have said about them and to them, or ridiculed them about what they wore or how they looked and I have had enough. I guess I have done nothing about that either and really want to be part of a solution. I'm actually doing this for me too. I have been too timid for too long and lived with this fear not to stand up for myself, so I would watch this happen to me and others and hoping things would be different, but not doing anything about it. I should have bopped you on the nose years ago. Sorry that's not the solution, but maybe I could have said something earlier. I want to be a stronger more proactive person and be able to look back and think I did something to honour my friend Josh. That's me!'

'OK, James, what about you?'

'Well, a bit like Taylor I have been bullied and seen others get bullied and I have sat silently doing nothing, but secretly hating it. I have even deliberately made jokes about myself so I could get in before the bullies did and I guess that shows them I'm OK with it, but I also realise I even encourage more of the behaviour and comments I actually hate, because I want to fit in. You probably suspect it but don't know, but yes, I am gay and have known for a while but only told a select few. I have been too scared that it would bring more negative attention to me and a lot have called me derogatory gay names anyway, so I just want to feel OK in my own skin and like Taylor, I want to be less timid, stand up for myself and others and be a part of the change that needs to happen at this school. I feel a little intimidated right now, truth be told, because both Steele and Chris you both know the things you have called me!, But I believe everyone deserves a second chance, so I'm hoping what you have both said is true, but the proof will be in the pudding as they say. Thanks, that's why I'm here.'

'Thanks, James, what about you Meg?' I ask, knowing what she's going to say because of our talk yesterday, but it's important the others know as well. She tells them about what she knows people say behind her back, and she is a bit more reserved saying that some of those people are in this group, but doesn't elaborate, but I can see three in this group who show signs of guilt. She goes on to explain about the exclusion and aloneness she feels at school and how that affects her whole life. She says she has no real friends and recognises that she has also chosen to distance herself, because she was fearful of being rejected by others, so doesn't give them a chance to actively reject her. I find this a bit sad as she is saying these things. She stops for a few seconds as the tears start to well up in her eyes and the emotions take hold. I go over to her and go to give her a hug and am surprised that everyone in the group go over and we have a group hug, which sort of makes us all laugh and breaks the sadness. I say, 'Meg, we HEAR you, we are here to make things right.' I think it's important for us to start sharing these experiences with others and get them to do the same. I don't think many of us know how much suffering, sadness and fear we actually create ourselves and impose on others, sometimes because we don't know how others are really feeling.

'Lucky last Andrew, why are you here?' I ask. Andrew says he has been bullied, but personally felt he could handle it and put up with it until he was able to leave school. He said he keeps to himself and a few friends and could go relatively unnoticed by the bullies, but the thing that has hurt him the most was when there had been a girl he thought was just the nicest person he knew at the school last year, but she was bullied by other students. He went on to say that he could see how this attractive, sporty, funny and genuinely good person was worn down by others. He said it all started with 1 of the cool guys at school trying to "hook up" with her and she rejected his advances, he then made up a name, calling her "Susie Soft Arse" which was a name he started spreading and within days a lot of other students were also calling her that and publicly saying it while she was there and hearing it.

Andrew became a bit emotional, going on to say how he could see the pain, shame and humiliation this person was feeling and how over the next couple of weeks she was a shadow of the bubbly person he knew before this all started. He said the students didn't let up either, they would call her that name any opportunity they got and he would see how depressed she had become in only a short time. He said it was heart-breaking for him to see, but like others had already mentioned he was too fearful to even offer her comfort or stand up for her because of not wanting to put himself in harm's way so he silently suffered inside, while she suffered. He said then one day she was gone, it was rumoured her parents took her out of the school and she went somewhere else. He said he hadn't seen her since, but did hear from someone that they saw her working in a clothing store, but he has been too embarrassed to look her up and go into the store, because she probably would not want to have anything to do with anyone from this school. Andrew was visibly upset and you could see how his body language showed he genuinely felt bad. He indicated he also wanted to be less fearful in general.

I thank Andrew and think from what a few have already said, I knew Josh wouldn't have been feeling well when he was going through his issues and my own fear of what could happen prevented me from being his friend. There are a number of reasons that fear exists and it has a lot to do with our social interactions and us, so wanting to fit in, that we choose not do the "right" thing. The stupid thing is, we only sort of guess what fitting in is. I mean let's face it, who really "decides" what's cool and why anything else is dorky or uncool. I have been thinking about this the last few days and I'm not sure, but maybe we can discuss some of this more, but I guess we all want to be part of a group, to your point Meg no one wants to be excluded, we would like to be included somehow. The problem is we tend to exclude, at least from our own little groups, people who are different to us. It's like there is a checklist and a hierarchy of inclusion, everyone wants to be part of the cool and popular group, or the sporty ones, who sometimes are both, and then there is that in between groups, not overly popular and then there others who are then put into the "different" categories, like the Goths or death metal crew. No matter what though, each of those groups has their "checklist" of rules to be part of that group. I can't see the Goths wanting to include any of the sporty students, because you never see any of them really doing anything sporty, so they probably "hang it" on each other if anyone within the group was doing anything outside of those rules.

We constantly pass judgement and give feedback to each other within the group as to why we should be or should not be associated with certain people. I knew early on that my group thought Josh was a dork. I heard them talk about him and when you guys would pick on him, as much as I felt bad for him, I also wanted to make sure the group thought I was one of them and thought the same as them, so I would laugh and say things behind his back to them I didn't really mean. I was actually being someone else to "fit in" and stay in with my group. I also had this worry that if I did side with Josh and the group decided I was "out", then who would I be with? I had the same fear of exclusion, because I have been there in Primary school, I had a nasty bunch of girls who excluded me in my final year and I would spend a lot of time by myself. It was a horrible 12 months for me and when I got here, it was like a whole new start. Anyway, enough about my little philosophy, let's talk about some kind of strategy for this group.

We all then head off our separate ways, but I decide to catch up with Andrew. I thank him for sharing his story and he says that he thinks about that girl pretty much every day and he feels disappointed in himself because he didn't do anything, not even a soothing word to help her when she was hurting. He says he found he was making himself depressed because he didn't consider himself worthy of being anyone's friend because he couldn't stand up for her or help her in any way and in the end, she had to go.

He says to make matters worse, even though he "knew" he was a bit nerdy, he said she was friendly to everyone and would come and talk to him and she was one of the few people who even showed him the time of day. He said Susie was the one silver lining he had to even come to school apart from the education side of things which he actually also liked. I do remember seeing him get academic awards and stuff at school assembly, but our group would make fun of that stuff behind his back.

I feel a tinge of guilt now given all that has happened and find my face start to flush with embarrassment just thinking about it. He goes on to say how when the taunts started, he was hoping it would just be a novelty and it would die off. He says he couldn't understand how 1 person could so quickly influence a whole lot of people and on someone who should have been one of the popular people, she was gorgeous, funny, smart, athletic and genuinely nice, but they had to find a way to bring her down. He said he just couldn't understand what they got out of it. We discuss that question briefly and decide to talk to the group tomorrow and tease it out a bit more. We then go our separate ways.

After I get home, I call Clint and we discuss how things are progressing. I tell him about the meeting and some of the stories the individuals shared. Clint's says he is quite impressed with what we have come up with and the fact that each of those group members felt good enough to share their reasons with the group. He says that is a great sign, because it means the members are having Blue Pool conversations, even with tough private information.

We talk a bit about wanting to fit in and not wanting to be excluded. He says because we have a natural instinct for Fight or Flight, there are undercurrents to our behaviour affected by this as we grow up, and it sits with this instinct, which ultimately is designed as a defence mechanism. There are two sides to this defence. One is Passive Defensive and the other is Aggressive Defensive. He indicates that there are some business tools that actually show how these undertones plays out in the workforce through interactions and ultimately people with these styles tend to be less effective.

He says I should read up a bit more on Human Synergistics, the Circumplex and the Lifestyle Inventory tool, which shows how this can have an impact on an individual and also how it then translates in a work environment. He goes on to say that the tool is designed for personal development and the background work he does, focuses on how people can become more "Blue" or more focused on Constructive Style Development, which he says ties in with his Blue Brain/ Red Brain and Full Metal Jacket program. He says there are a number of common themes of people behaviour which are linked to this "undercurrent" of the fight or flight reflex. I look some of this up.

(Scan the QR code or hold down Ctrl and click the link)

http://www.human-synergistics.com.au/about-us/the-circumplex

Chapter 37

Thursday comes around pretty quick, I have been talking a fair bit in between to M1 and Taylor and I am really starting to like them both a lot. M1 has changed significantly and she is a much nicer person than she was before. I did also talk to the other group members a bit more since we started the group. In our meeting we each throw ideas of what we should or could do to make things change. A lot of good ideas are brought forward, but the short version is this, we all agree we need to do some work to help each individual deal with things better, we thought that some awareness training like the Red Brain Blue Brain stuff is helpful, maybe also learning some techniques to move them into a Blue Space when things happen. I suggested the Tips for Negative thoughts stuff I found on the net and maybe even having information sessions where others can share how they dealt with things when they were going through a tough time, or maybe even get information from someone like Steele who was a bully and he has seen the error of his ways and the effect Josh's death had on him.

We said once we focused on how to help an individual to be more robust, we would then focus on making people aware of how the group and others affect what we do and think. This is where we would consider talking about the effects of the bystander effect, or other psychological biases we as humans have and the effects these can have if we are not aware of it. We agreed we need to explore some of these areas a bit more. We also agreed that somehow, we need to involve the teachers and also the parents, because often a lot of what we learn early on is coming from home and if the behaviour and role models are bad, then it will make the job harder to change behaviour. We are not sure what that type of work would look like but put it in the "parking lot" for further discussion later.

We start to discuss how we take initiative by taking on the Politicians and the Education Department to change the system? This idea also has some merit we could potentially say that it's the students who are dictating what needs to change in our school, to reduce bullying and drop outs and obesity and teen suicide.

The students have a say in what programs get introduced and considered. There was potential for the "us" VS "the system" as a point to unite the students. We would then explore the opportunities to get more involved and offer innovative ideas of how to improve our schools and look at different learning methods and different curriculum and some form of innovation going forward. This was starting to take shape. I could feel the groups energy and enthusiasm spring up, we could see various possibilities to get more involved in the group activities, if the activities were to be seen as "revolutionary" and cool at the same time.

The outcome is still to have a great school culture where everyone takes care of each other but we would be trying to get the Education Department and politicians to change some of their regimented views and implement some new ideas to change the school culture. We knew we couldn't do this alone, but we wanted some say to highlight what areas they should be working on.

I decide to stop the meeting, but now there is some real excitement behind this. I suggest that maybe over the next week we get into pairs and explore some options around this idea. I ask who they want to work with and I am a little surprised when Steele offers to work with Taylor. He jokingly says he will wear some protective headwear. She doesn't look overly impressed but doesn't say no. The rest of the group pairs off and I'm working with Meg.

I look through the stuff we put together and I can see a connection with the Circumplex stuff Clint told me to look at. I see that the Red and Green "Defensive Styles" play out in the behaviour of the stories each of the students have told.

If you are in fear, you tend to be the Green style, which the material describes as "Self-protecting, being good, retroactive, inactive, avoiding risk and has Depression in terms of individual wellbeing".

The Red style is Self-Promoting, Looking Good, Reactive, Counteractive, Seeking Risk, Competing and has Anxiety in terms of individual wellbeing.

The Blue Style is Self-Enhancing, Doing Good, Proactive, Interactive, Managing Uncertainty, Collaborating and is Optimistic.

I can see that we would want to work on getting everyone into the Blue space.

Chapter 38

I was a bit taken aback when Steele nominated, he wanted to work with me when Emily asked if we could work in pairs. I actually find him quite witty and he has a good sense of humour, but only time will tell if he does what he said he would do and then sustain it. Even though it was a surprise, I think he's quite good looking so it might not be all bad.

As the group breaks, I ask him to stay back so we can talk. He stays back and when everyone is out of the room, I ask him why he chose to work with me. He says, 'Well, I know you will be honest with me and I also know you were good friends with Josh, so I would like to at least find out some things about him and you in terms of how I may have affected him and others in the school. I know some of the others have said things, but you have not only said things, you even physically assaulted me! Maybe I'm a glutton for punishment, but I thought you might be able to help me understand things better.'

I say, 'Well if you ever need someone to punch you on the nose, I'm happy to volunteer my time.'

'Seriously though, I see you have been trying and you appear to be on the level. I just hope this is not just some act you put on because you still feel a little guilty and then a month or two down the track the pain in the arse Steele comes out again. If that happens, expect more punches, or maybe I will learn some more elaborate moves and pop your eye out with a chopstick or something like that.' We walk off and have some fairly light conversation about things and then go our separate ways. I do see a guy who appears to be trying and he is quite easy to talk to once you get to know him.

I go home and I decide to contact Clint as he may be able to give me some ideas or some information to help. I tell him about our meeting and the discussions which seem to be around helping individuals and groups to give feedback and trying to get them to encourage good behaviour. I ask him if he has any ideas. He tells me to read a book called *The One Minute Manager* by Blanchard and Johnson.

(Scan the QR code or hold down Ctrl and click the link)

http://www.amazon.com/The-Minute-Manager-Kenneth-Blanchard/dp/0688014291

He says although it's a book meant to be based around management, it is quite short and very simple around feedback. I download an electronic copy. It really is quite a simple book and in short makes three important points. One is setting goals and the other two revolve around giving feedback or as the book explains it as the One Minute Praising and the One Minute Reprimand. The key around each of the feedback is that people know they will be getting feedback and the feedback needs to be immediate. When giving the negative one, it is clear that you need to reassure the person this is not about them as a person, just the behaviour which may not be good. I definitely see that these simple ideas could be used when we start setting up the intervention to change the student's behaviour at school.

I can see that we need to get people to the point where we all agree on what behaviour we want and then "reinforce" the good behaviour with the praise and "reduce" the bad behaviour by using the reprimand, but focusing on the behaviour not the person. I can see ways we can apply these simple rules, but we need to address the "why" people are not doing that already.

Chapter 39

Steele and I talk a fair bit on Facebook over the next day and we agree to catch up a couple of days later, I've done a fair bit of reading on Change Management and Beliefs, which was actually interesting. We choose to meet at a restaurant, I felt the need to at least make an effort and so I bought a new outfit. I find myself attracted to him, I'm not sure he feels the same way, so I don't want to make it too obvious, obviously me showing how I feel to guys is not my strong point. I will see what he does. I find it hard to be angry at him, I think I am starting to believe his intent to want to make things right. But I am still guarded about him, the reason we are even interacting is because of Josh's death and when I think of that, I get a sharp pang run through me and I feel an element of guilt, but then I also understand he wanted us to do something and I feel a bit better.

When we meet in the restaurant, it looks like he has also made an effort, he seems to be more dressed up than I have seen him before and I feel myself smiling on the inside, *maybe he likes me?* I think. He seems to be smiling from ear to ear and I ask him why he's so happy. He says he suddenly feels more energy and feels like all our group activity and even our interaction has given him something better to focus on, rather than what he had been focussed on before we all met the first time. He surprises me when he kisses me on the cheek. I feel myself blushing a little, he doesn't seem to notice, and he seems quite excited about information he has sourced for the group.

We talk a little about what we have been doing, I tell him what I found on change management and beliefs and he tells me he has been reading about the "Bystander effect" and why people don't step in to help others when there are other people around. He goes further to say that when people don't step in it actually also has an effect on those involved. As it almost gives the impression, they are condoning the behaviour. He goes on to say, this does two things, it reinforces the bad behaviour from the perpetrator and also says to the victim that they have no support. In a nutshell, 'Doing nothing is doing something.'

I explain to him about the *One Minute Manager* and its three points, in addition I explain another book I read called *Kluge* by Gary Marcus.

(Scan the QR code or hold down Ctrl and click the link)

http://klugethebook.com/

In this book he writes about beliefs and how we are wired to be easily fooled. He talks about the "Halo Effect" which is where we might associate one positive trait with everything about the person being positive, such as an attractive person also being fun, nice and honest when all you actually know is their looks. The opposite is also present, where because of one negative thing we make negative generalisations about them without actual fact.

Another interesting thing he mentions is about the reflexive system of the brain, which is what Clint calls Red Brain and the Deliberative System, which is what Clint calls Blue Brain. He makes an important point that when we are stressed, tired or distracted our Blue Brain is the first to go, leaving us to function using the Red Brain. Steele and I discuss this for a little while, how when you are really tired you do become irritable and prone to being angry. We laugh a bit when we use examples of ourselves and our families that confirm this idea. It's actually quite funny how we all react when we are a bit tired or stressed.

Steele tells me he has also been reading a book called *What Makes Us Tick?*

(Scan the QR code or hold down Ctrl and click the link)

https://www.amazon.com.au/What-Makes-Us-Tick-desires-ebook/dp/B006FLJVOE

He found some interesting ideas, one in particular was how parents try to "protect" their children so much that it can actually lead to other problems if you don't allow them to experience life in general. We talk about that for a while and agree that even the schools try to "protect" students by not wanting them to feel bad if they don't win a race, so everybody gets a ribbon for competing, but then kids don't learn how to deal with some disappointment and then when they get older they have an entitlement mentality and expect things to fall into place and if it doesn't go their way, they have no coping skills and end up having bigger problems.

It reminds me of an awesome interview.

(Scan the QR code or hold down Ctrl and click the link)

https://www.facebook.com/smizzymusic/videos/10154718480226427/

We take down some notes to take back to the group tomorrow. Steele suddenly stops and becomes quite serious. He asks me how I feel about what he did to Josh now and what I think about what he has been trying to do to rectify things. I think briefly and advise him I still have some anger towards what happened with him and Josh, but I also acknowledge that reading some of these books and being part of this group has opened my eyes to how these type of interactions are probably more typical and many others contribute to that type of behaviour continuing. I finish off by telling him I am impressed by the way he has conducted himself since he came back to school and appeared to take responsibility for his part and also for putting forward his intent to rectify the situation.

He looks right at me and smiles, he takes my hand and I start to feel a bit excited and my stomach does a backflip. I'm suddenly self-conscious and find myself playing with my hair and feeling rather flushed in the face. I can feel my face heat up and I know I must be turning very red. He must have sensed my feeling and lets go of my hand and just says thank you for what I said about recognising his effort.

We make some more small talk and ask each other some questions about each other and are quite surprised that we like similar music and also UFC. We talk a bit about that and who our favourite fighters are. It turns out we are both fans of Robert "The Reaper" Whittaker. We question each other a bit more and I start to sense that I'm starting to like Steele a bit more. I still have a little bit of nervousness about him, but it's quickly evaporating. When we eventually leave, I feel a little sad and I start to look more intently at him to see if there is any indication of what he might think about me.

He does kiss me goodbye on the cheek, but I'm not sure if it means anything and for the rest of the afternoon, I try to replay events in my head to see if I can pick anything up. Him holding my hand, me blushing like Rudolf's nose and him kissing my cheek, lots of things to take in, but still too many questions. I found myself doing this same thing when I was trying to figure out what Josh thought of me and so many times, I got to the brink of asking him out but backed down because of the fear that he wouldn't feel the same way, so I lived in this self-imposed twisted agony. As I'm thinking I guess I would rather bear humiliation than not knowing, or so I fleetingly think, but now faced with the same situation, I still can't overcome the fear of humiliation, so I convince myself I need to wait to see if Steele makes any moves. I don't like this thought all that much but I am OK to wait and see. Again I torture myself.

Chapter 40

The group get together and everyone's quite excited and we brainstorm our ideas that we have researched and what we think could be helpful in terms of what we want to do. We decide to just list them and see what is best. The list goes:

- Wilful Blindness
- Feedback methods
- Red Brain / Blue Brain
- Making someone more robust rather than sheltering them
- Social interactions and our thoughts
- Negative thinking
- Positive Psychology
- Schools and developing good culture
- Change Management
- Group Dynamics
- How beliefs are formed
- Root cause analysis

We are quite excited about the list and talk about the reasons and the priority for putting each one up. We all agree that root cause analysis should be the start, so we can try to work out what is causing this bullying and bad relationships and causing students to hate themselves, to pick on others and why it continues.

This is also where we think Change Management is important, because once we know the causes, we need to consider methods that can help to make the changes. We acknowledge we don't know much about that, so we need to go and find out a bit more.

We felt the others were quite similar in the sense that it either focuses on helping the individual to maybe dealing with things better or to help group interactions. They were also different in subtle ways, so they each needed to at least be understood and considered in terms of how they fit into the root causes and how we then look at strategies to change those things that need to be changed.

So, we all agree to go out and see what we can find on root cause analysis and also change management. We agree to let each other know what we find and what we will explore so that we are not doubling up looking at the same things.

Chapter 41

Checking through the net we come across Six Sigma's *5 Whys*, which is basically asking why a few times when faced with a problem, we look at a number of different ones, but this seems the most simple and when we apply it to our problems it reveals what we think are the root causes of those things. The technique is explained below.

5 Whys:

(Scan the QR code or hold down Ctrl and click the link)

http://www.isixsigma.com/tools-templates/cause-effect/determine-root-cause-5-whys/

When we applied this to Josh's suicide, it worked something like this.

1. Why did Josh commit suicide?
   Answer: Because he was depressed.

2. Why was he depressed?
   Answer: Because he was picked on.

3. Why was he picked on?
   Answer: Because Steele decided to pick on him.

4. Why did Steele do that?
   Answer: Because we all encouraged it and no one stepped in to stop it.
5. Why did we encourage it and no one stepped in to stop it?
   Answer: We didn't take into account how he felt about it and some were too scared to step in.

6. Why didn't we take into account how he felt about it and why were some of us too scared to step in?
   Answer: Because no one really has been taught to put ourselves in others shoes and we were scared it might have turned on us.

7. Why has no one really been taught to put themselves in others shoes and why were we scared it might have turned on us?
   Answer: School and parents have not thought to be deliberate about teaching us this and also not encouraging us to share with each other how we actually do feel about this. Also parents tend to encourage a "selfish" mentality because they want the best for their own kids, but even at the expense of others. Maybe there are other reasons this might happen but we are not sure.

We went beyond the 5 Whys and that apparently is OK, but we also know it's not quite the end maybe there are other reasons, but we don't know enough to actually do full root cause analysis. As we explore these things, we might actually come up with other causes. We might also be able to get others who know more about these things to help us too like Clint, but we were reasonably happy with what we started with.

We tease out the final answer a bit more, around teachers and parents not being deliberate about teaching us about considering others and making each other aware of what we are really feeling. We agree that we need to at least talk to the school about doing something in this space. We aren't sure what exactly but it's something we want to raise.

Chapter 42

We found this short clip which gives a little insight into what we could do if people felt OK to speak up and share things they wouldn't discuss. It also gives another perspective on interacting with people different to us.

Dare to disagree:

(Scan the QR code or hold down Ctrl and click the link)

http://www.ted.com/talks/margaret_heffernan_dare_to_disagree.html

We all agree that Clint is correct about this dialogue stuff that we need to focus on getting students feeling comfortable talking to anyone about things that bother them and also for others on the outside also saying things when they think things are not right. We actually talk about why his Red Brain/Blue Brain stuff makes sense, because it brings into our awareness why we don't have these conversations and it also makes us think about what we can do to help with making our fellow students feel OK to do that more.

We start to brainstorm about what it takes to create a "great" person. In the end we come to the conclusion that is takes a community to educate a child. We start to think around who exactly is the "community"?

The list starts with:

- Parents and immediate family.
- Kindergarten teachers and other students.
- School teachers and other students.
- Friends outside of school, such as sporting teammates etc.
- Anyone else you are likely to come into contact with.
- Rules and regulations from Government have an impact, or at least "try" to regulate behaviour.

Our thinking starts to go to a combination of what "should" individuals know about themselves? What should groups know about the social impacts they have on others? How do we influence the people listed above to teach and reinforce their children and others to know and apply that knowledge? We also talk a bit about the

Human Synergistics stuff, where we discuss that those people with more Blue, are what you would consider good leaders, who are comfortable in their own skins and are about helping everyone achieve and not just them.

Chapter 43

We talk about various change management models, but the one we liked and which fit in with what we brainstormed was from a book *Influencer: The power to change anything*.

We find someone's blog who had gone through the training based on this book and his summary is pretty good, it outlines the 3-step process, which is

1. Clarify measurable results.
2. Find Vital behaviours.
3. Use six sources of influence.

He covers this off in more detail in the link:

(Scan the QR code or hold down Ctrl and click the link)

http://sourcesofinsight.com/influencer-the-power-to-change-anything/

The important discussion points for us is the notion around "Vital Behaviour". It's like root cause behaviour in our view. If you behaved this way, you are more likely to get a better result.

The other real key was the six sources of influence, which is:

1. Personal Motivation: Do they want to engage in the behaviour?
2. Personal Ability: Do they have the knowledge, skills and strengths to do the right things even when it's hardest?
3. Social Motivation: Are other people encouraging the right behaviour and discouraging the wrong?
4. Social Ability: Do others provide the help, information and resource required at particular times?
5. Structural Motivation: Are rewards, pay promotions, performance reviews, perks or costs encouraging the right behaviours or discouraging the wrong?
6. Structural Ability: Are there enough clues to stay on course? Does the environment (tools, facilities, information, reports, proximity to others, policies) enable the right behaviours or discourage the wrong?

We start to brainstorm what do we need to do to get everyone personally motivated? We discuss the day that we all met in the lecture theatre and how we had people like Steele and Emily stand up and talk to the group. We felt we needed to appeal to all those who were bullied or who witnessed bullying but didn't like it. We needed to appeal to those who really wanted to see a change.

Then we needed to think of ways we could increase their personal ability to be involved in the changes. We thought giving them information and making them personally aware of some of the stuff Clint mentioned and also giving them skills to be able to discuss things with others when they didn't like that other person's behaviour.

In terms of the social motivation we thought we needed to work on how we get the student group, teachers and parents encouraging the right behaviour and discouraging the wrong ones. We talk a bit about this and that "selfish" view that our parents want us to do well, but even at the expense of others, we thought we need to work on how we can work at all of us doing well. We also felt that schools want their students to get good results, so they put all their energy into the "good" students, who may be academically better. We thought this is an area we might be able to use the group to help each other out by getting the teachers and school using group methods better. We thought this then led into the Social Ability space.

We felt the school, or more specifically the Education Department needed to consider a more group focussed approach to Education and somehow try to influence what parents are doing before children get to school age. This sounded like a big piece of work, but we thought we would put it on the table and explore further later.

We talked about what we could do in terms of the structural motivation space. We talked about our current reward systems which is about highlighting those who do well academically and sports wise. We also talked about how a lot of students are made to feel bad by others for doing well academically, by being called a dork or brown nose and lots of other things which actually inhibit others wanting to do well. It's like the environment or culture makes being "dumb" cool and being smart almost "uncool". We can understand that there is a dilemma on wanting to "fit" in and also doing well at school.

We decide to apply the 5 Whys to this issue.

1. Why do students want being academically good to be uncool?
   Answer: Because if they are not good academically or they don't want to put in the work then they want to say negative things about others to sort of deflect negativity from themselves. In a way it's better to justify not doing well academically by "convincing" yourself that you didn't really want to do well.

2. Why do they want to deflect negativity from themselves?
   Answer: Doing this can make them feel a bit better about themselves and if others "join" them they feel they have social support and they are part of the "in" group.

3. Why do they want to be part of the "in" group?
   Answer: Everyone wants to feel like they belong and no one wants to feel alienated, so they tend to pick a group to belong to.

We aren't too sure if this is a good answer but decide to explore this a bit further. We all talk about how we really want to be accepted. I look around the group and we are from different backgrounds and groups and yet I'm a little overwhelmed by how we all really just want to be accepted. I listen as each of us talk about why this is important to us. I hear things like acceptance of the group is the most important thing. It is like our identity. Yes, we are individuals, but we all feel our individual happiness and self-worth is linked to where we feel we belong. We all said we didn't want to be alone. We would all love to have no "set" groups and to have everyone included. It sounds like an unattainable goal, but we also talk a lot about who actually determines what and who is cool or not, and we say it's us!

We start to ask some questions about how we can actually have an impact on changing the student's views on each other and try to think of ways to break down those groups and barriers which keep those groups quite separated. We begin to discuss what the Vital behaviours would need to be to see any changes. We list the following:

- Everyone needs to challenge behaviour that keeps the divisions up.
- It needs to be consistent: See something then do something!
- Once someone says something, others should also show obvious support.
- The way it is said needs to be constructive and done well.
- We need to proactively include others into the group and be welcoming to anyone who comes in.

The discussion goes around these points for a while and Steele points out that there does need to be an intervention where all the students are advised of this plan, so we are all on the same page and so as many as possible know to say something when they see something. In addition we know we need to do the dialogue model work with everyone, so they know how to have the good conversations.

We also think the teachers need to be able to run the training and incorporate it into the lessons and especially run classes for new students who are just starting. They also need to be explained the "new rules" of the way things are at our school. We say that we need to have like ambassadors at the school who welcome the little ones and show them around, introduce them to others and genuinely include them and also "show" them how it is to be one of the Blu Kru! Which was a name we threw around for the group. We aren't convinced that will stay that way, but it is what we call it for now.

Chapter 44

I meet with the students and they outline what they had been discussing and some of it makes me think about decision making and wanting to fit in and how we feel. I decide to look into this a bit more. As much as I have been using my Red Brain Blue Brain program for a little while, it focuses quite broadly on the Physiological components for ease of explanation to others. I have this feeling I need to research a bit more detail to help explain some of their questions.

I have a flick through this awesome book I mentioned previously again to refresh my memory.

You Are the Placebo by Dr Joe Dispenza.

(Scan the QR code or hold down Ctrl and click the link)

https://www.hayhouse.com/you-are-the-placebo

The nutshell version of the book is he explains how our thoughts can have an effect on our biology both negatively and positively. He explains how our experiences and consequence thoughts can make our bodies react in a consistent manner and "form" the way we will react.

I start to think about how we can use this information to "shape" how children and teens develop through the school years in a proactive and deliberate way. It comes to me when I make a lot of the connections in my head that we need to set good routines for the very young students, we need to focus on the positive psychology and also some kind of meditation practices, so that they are getting deliberate practice at skills of the mind which will help them deal with life's challenges and also develop better school relationships, with less destructive presences.

As I'm working on this, I see on the news that a young girl called Dolly, who had been in an advertisement has committed suicide due to bullying.

(Scan the QR code or hold down Ctrl and click the link)

https://www.news.com.au/lifestyle/real-life/news-life/dolly-everetts-parents-reveal-what-led-to-their-daughters-death/news-story/b7984758aa1ce96def787ad0c20cde93

The whole thing just makes me sad, because like Josh she couldn't see a way out and felt this was the best option. I decide I can't just wait and do this work at one school, so I create a Group Facebook Page and call it the Blue Flame Project to promote "spreading blue brain thoughts". The intent is to get some feedback on this book which I have now put together, even though it is incomplete at this point of creating the Page, I think there may be enough in it to at least get people thinking about the different ways to deal with this issue.

I get some good initial responses and posts and add some additional posts that I think might help too. I also included a couple of videos I did when some of the Army Veterans I had worked with were raising suicide awareness and I put these on as a way of people being more aware of how they think and use some strategies to help them.

I start to strategize about how I can use my rehabilitation methods in a more proactive way rather than in an after-the-fact way I used to. I also need to update and consider some of the new neuroscience stuff I have been reading about since I last did rehabilitation over ten years ago.

As I'm doing it, this reminds me of a couple of articles I read on teaching Norms in a business environment, but ultimately this is important at school level too, as we ultimately need to set the tone for what the behaviour is we want to see, also the teachers would be taught how to do this and ultimately they set expectations, they use the students, who are taught and have facilitated Blue Pool Conversations to help calibrate the behaviour they are trying to implement.

How to create Executive Team Norms:

(Scan the QR code or hold down Ctrl and click the link)

https://hbr.org/2018/01/how-to-create-executive-team-norms-and-make-them-stick?utm_campaign=hbr&utm_source=twitter&utm_medium=social

I also think about how I am going to incorporate the information that shows how much of an effect Dopamine has on us and essentially millennials even more so because of technology. I am dealing with a different person than the 40-plus-year-olds who got injured while working. I'm dealing with much younger people, whose brains are not fully formed, but who have access to instant technology at a very early age. This video about the millennials is again appropriate here as well.

(Scan the QR code or hold down Ctrl and click the link)

https://www.facebook.com/smizzymusic/videos/10154718480226427/?fref=gs&dti=2013810215498734&hc_location=group

The next step is to see how to use this along with some of the other studies and books that cover how we make decisions.

Chapter 45

We meet with Clint and the small group of students. Clint advises that he was saddened by a suicide he heard about on the news of a young girl named Dolly who had committed suicide due to bullying as well. He says he has created a Facebook Group called, "The Blue Flame Project". He says its purpose is to not just create awareness but to give people strategies to deal with this. He says we need different strategies for schools and for the community and then also look at interventions based on age, as there are different brain states based on our maturity.

We talk about his refined Full Mental Jacket Program, which he says is a combination of helping the individual understand their brains and thoughts a lot better, as well as how we make decisions in a little more depth. He says this information is targeted at someone that is an adult, as they need to understand the information, whereas with children the teachers need to understand this part and create "lessons and activities" that allow for these areas to be developed more proactively. Clint says he started to check out issues with the education system and come across this, which is food for thought on what the structure of lessons and lectures.

Six Problems with Modern Schools.

(Scan the QR code or hold down Ctrl and click the link)

https://www.facebook.com/greatbigminds/videos/334919270244966/

Clint also points out some things to consider as Principal and reading the article I see as leader of the school; I do need to be brave on this and that the hierarchy are risk averse. I guess when I think about it they stay that way because they think we are doing well, and year upon year we compare ourselves to our previous year's performance and how we compare to other schools who are also using the same Education System, but because we have more funding we can do more things, but not really performing that much better in the grand scheme of things. The innovation checklist does give me some things to think about.

School Innovation Checklist.

(Scan the QR code or hold down Ctrl and click the link)

https://www.linkedin.com/pulse/school-innovation-checklist-2018-paul-kidson/?trackingId=MgjDkkML9en9j5OkkconUw%3D%3D

This one is also interesting about taking some action on what we watch and read. Brainwashed.

https://www.facebook.com/RobDialJr/videos/1860609730623165/

Chapter 46

I'm back at home and quite reflective and trying to strategize a bit more on what I can do to help the school and these individuals even more. The Dolly suicide makes me think about Josh and I start to think back of some things I learned during my studies around profiling and how investigators would look at a crime scene and then try to piece through and work out what the person was thinking at various stages, to get a better sense of who this person is most likely to be.

I think a similar process may be helpful to piece together a "potential" timeline of events and get a sense of what events took place and at the same time work out what the person was thinking in response. From there we could work out the psychological components and thoughts that then were occurring as that was happening. This could also allow us to potentially guess what may have been happening at a physiological level as it was taking place.

I start to think through some of the events in Josh's life which I'm aware of, such as his dad leaving or more like abandoning him, through no fault of his own and then at the same time he had to fend for himself and look after his mother. Then essentially having to leave their house and change schools, all in a very small space of time. Let's think this through.

- Mum finds out Dad is having an affair and confronts him, there is obvious fighting going on around this, and dad gets angry and decides to move out. He shows no affection for Josh and never tries to console him or comfort him and reassure him. Josh's thinking must have been: *My dad is leaving my mum; hopefully when he gets his new place, I can visit and see him.* This doesn't happen and as time goes on, he starts to feel abandoned by his dad, because frankly he is. Feeling worthless and not loved would be devastating to a young child, especially given that apparently they had a pretty good relationship. His dad was, from all appearances, a good father and husband and it was totally out of the blue, the whole affair and then the complete walkout.
- Couple this with Vicki's response to her husband leaving, which was a complete meltdown according to her. She wasn't looking after herself or Josh, to the point that he was looking after her. So he is essentially abandoned by Dad and has to deal with that, but he is getting no support from the other caregiver so what do I think he is feeling at this stage? I can only imagine the internal dialogue in his head which would be along the lines of, 'Why would Dad just walk out and not even care about me at all?' You could assume that if he replayed this discussion in his head it would invoke red brain responses, such as sadness, some shame (perceived)

because of his feeling of not being seen as relevant to this person who was such a big factor in his life up to that point. If he was to be repeatedly thinking these things without anyone trying to help him, he would potentially play the repeat red brain loop and slowly but surely red brain chemical responses would be rising and he would potentially get to a point that his neurons are wiring and firing together in this pattern and he starts to form a pattern of habitual thinking of this worthlessness. In this case, there is no one saying he is worthless, but his dad leaving and choosing to never contact him again, makes him think he is worthless and he has a massive sense of loss, but his loss is his dad's choice and that causes pain.

- So he's now looking after Vicki and not long after they are forced to move from a house and area he loves and so there is unwanted change, which can be tough even without the impetus of his dad leaving. Again there is a sense of loss and he is getting no support, so his own thought pattern from earlier is red brain thoughts and his body chemistry is changing because he is "stuck" in that thought pattern and every time he asks himself questions, such as 'Why did Dad abandon me?' or 'Did I matter that little to him that it was so easy to run away and not even look back?' He will be activating that Red Brain cascade and then he "feels" bad and it affects his body chemistry even more. This cycle starts to become a habit. Which goes a bit like this: (Apologies if it is oversimplified but it does help understand it.)
    1. He has the thought. His brain creates a neurotransmitter and a neuropeptide and sends a message to the body. His body responds by having a "feeling". The brain detects that the body is having a "feeling" and it generates another thought matched to that exact feeling that will produce more of the same chemical messages that allows him to think the way he was just feeling. In a nutshell, thinking creates feelings which creates thinking equal to that feeling. So in Josh's case when his dad left, his thought may have been that he felt abandoned, which produced the sequence of little events in his body outlined above. This led him to feeling sad and this created the thought of being sad. If he then thinks the same thing again, it will perform the same sequence and the same thoughts usually produce the same feeling or emotion. If he now stays in that thought loop, this starts to become a bit more hardwired until it starts to become a habit and if he does it continually, the body becomes subconsciously conditioned to become its own mind. This pattern is now much harder to break, because the body and brain are responding much more automatically.
    2. The key now is how we can "arrest" the thought pattern before it becomes "hardwired" and habitual. Obviously, we can't ever stop bad things happening to us, but we need to be able to help these young people to deal with these things in a more positive way. The key is to be able to detach the real event from the future memories of that event, so they can "process" the memory differently so that other neurons are firing rather than the same neurons in the same pattern they are when they first experienced it.

I am starting to feel a bit tired, but all these thoughts about how we end up being the people we are and how we learn and understand our own emotions and how that affects our behaviour is intriguing. I start to think about my own childhood back in South Africa, I was brought up in a religious household, and while my parents weren't super strict there was certainly very little tolerance for being naughty or disrespectful. One of the biggest influences in my life was actually my grandmother on my mother's side. She always seemed to have time for others and her brother, who was my great uncle was very selfless and did a lot of work in the church and genuinely loved helping people. My grandmother used to make sandwiches for the needy, even though she herself wasn't exactly rich. She expected nothing in return, but often they would come and do "unrequested" yard and gardening work for her as a token of their appreciation. I do miss her as I'm thinking about her and I get a little nostalgic and think of all the times she used to look after me when I was on school holidays and my parents had to work. I have a few tears in my eyes as I think of her. I do miss her so much even though she has passed as long as I have been in Australia, which is just over 35 years. It is time for bed now, I am quite tired but feeling good about the progress we are making and the fact that we have multiple groups working on this even the students, which I think is great.

Chapter 47

It's been a few days since we all caught up with Clint at our principal's office and our little group has been teasing out some of the things Clint has mentioned. We explore his Facebook page which he recently set up.

We like the idea of the page and try to think of ways we could leverage the message it is sending. First, we think we need to make sure as many people we know are made aware of the page. We like the idea of them using the page to maybe set an event or even a concert with a key message around suicide prevention and also about bullying.

We discuss that The Blue Flame Project is a good enough name for the project, given Clint's explanation of why he came up with that name, which was to promote Blue Brain knowledge one person at a time and he likened it to starting a small flame hoping it would spread. We like the fact we can use the page to add content we feel is helpful and may stimulate thought on initiatives that can help. There are already some posts on there from some of the members and a few have said they have started reading the E-book.

As we are talking about these things, Andrew breaks some pretty big news. He said since we started this, he has looked up where Susie worked and has made contact with her. He said that it continued to eat at him that he didn't do anything to help her, because he was scared. He goes on to say how he would replay in his head those weeks of her being laughed at and teased. He says just looking at her crying with a look of disbelief that there were so many people on board and teasing her was not something he would ever forget. He says it still makes him feel nauseous inside. However since he has been working with the group, he has been trying to toughen himself up and asked some tough questions of himself.

Andrew goes on to say that the more he thought about it, the more he realised the shame of his inaction has stopped him from trying to find her, even just to make sure that she was OK. He said he was still shit scared inside, but pushed his fear aside for once and went to look her up. He said, she was working at a clothing store and when she saw him, she recognised him and her eyes lit up as she was so happy to see him. He said he was so excited to see her and her response. They got talking briefly and he told her how sorry he was with the way she had been treated and also how sorry he was that she had to leave. He said she indicated she was fine and had enjoyed the school she had ended up at, which was a little different to a normal traditional school and was more like a university kind of environment and she was looking to finish a course in Media and IT, which are things she is passionate about. He says he has asked her to go out with him and she agreed to catch up this weekend. His whole face was like the Cheshire cat as he grinned from ear to ear. The whole group erupted with genuine excitement for him.

We have a lot of questions for him. He says once he had broken the ice and saw her initial response, he said he was so scared to ask her, for fear of rejection, but then just remembered the stuff he had heard others in this group share and how they had missed opportunities, so he just went for it and asked her and now he couldn't be happier. He says he is quite proud of himself but is also thankful of how the group and the sharing of genuine stories had helped him realise he wasn't alone in how he felt and while it is good to have people that support you, he felt some of the initiatives and actions to help change our thoughts is what ultimately helped him get past the fear of shame and then the fear of rejection. He says in the end his fear of not knowing was greater than if she said no, but lucky for him it was a yes. We are all very excited for him as he explains where he is planning to take her.

After the excitement dies down a bit, we discuss some of the things we have been working on. I raise a posting from Will Smith, where he talks about Fault vs. Responsibility.

Fault vs. Responsibility:

Scan the QR code or hold down Ctrl and click the link)

https://www.facebook.com/uniladmag/videos/4366567730032919/

We all agree that is food for thought and that when you think about it, things will happen to us, but if we consider how Josh had responded, he certainly has looked at it from the fault side and couldn't find a way for him to take that responsibility for doing something to help himself. We discuss this and conclude that again it is a red brain thought to be stuck in that mentality, whereas Will says, he was in survival mode. From what we have read and heard from Clint, when we are in Fight or Flight mode, it is survival mode and we have various body chemical reactions and our brainwaves are at a faster pace than when we are relaxed.

We agree that if we and the school want to help the existing students, then there needs to be a focus on how we can help them to be able to change their focus from survival mode to having that mentality of being in control and being able to take responsibility for making changes that help ourselves. We also agree it is easier said than done, but we see how having a blue brain response, which is solution focused is what can help a person think their way out of that survival mode. We see that any interventions or small changes that can interrupt a long-term red brain response is the key. We understand that these emotions are part of our lives and there is nothing bad about having these emotions, we simply can't be happy all the time, but we don't want those emotions to become a central part of our lives, because it does have a detrimental effect on us. I read a saying, which sums it up nicely, *'No one ever drowned by falling in the water, they drown by staying there.'* I also think about a woman who summed up the issue of emotions very nicely. It is not about always being able to put aside these emotions, like sadness, anger and grief, but to be able to experience them, understand them and be able to do something positive with them.

Or if that is not an option, then at least don't allow it to be the only thing you focus on.

I also tell them about the interview I came across about the Millennials and it has some very good points about socials skills and patience and also using social media and smart phones less, so we can deliberately form relationships and increase those social skills.

Millennials:

(Scan the QR code or hold down Ctrl and click the link)

https://www.facebook.com/smizzymusic/videos/10154718480226427/

We talk about this a little and form the view that these are skills that schools need to focus on more than in the past, because we are all kind of hooked on our phones and it's likely to get worse if we let it. We talk about what he says about parents wanting to "protect" their kids and progress them even if they have not earnt it. We see that this is an issue, especially the part about getting a participation ribbon for something even when you come last. We start talking about how that would actually contribute to an "entitlement" view. We feel that if underneath it all, if you don't feel you deserve something then you would feel worse inside. Also, if you are getting better grades than you deserve continually, you probably do have an overinflated view of yourself and then when you do come up against disappointment, you aren't equipped to deal with that disappointment and then things can turn ugly.

Negative Emotions.

(Scan the QR code or hold down Ctrl and click the link)

https://www.facebook.com/TED/videos/10159946160830652/

Steele says he was reading an article on rewiring the brain through positive thought. It is evident that it ties in with Clint's Full Mental Jacket Program, because it is about giving the person pointers to interrupt a red brain response to something, not suppress it, but deal with it in a different way. It also shows how the thoughts diary he had Steele do, actually has some practical application and in essence is about trying to break the repeated wiring and firing of the same neurons, and altering the response.

Positive thinking rewires your brain.

(Scan the QR code or hold down Ctrl and click the link)

https://www.stevenaitchison.co.uk/how-positive-thinking-re-wires-your-brain/

We feel like we are progressing, we believe we need to be somehow setting activities or as Clint calls them routines, that causes the students to understand a component of their own psychology and how that can inhibit the conversations they should have with each other, which allows them to understand each other and forces them to interact more, but also that teachers can facilitate these discussions so that the students can find better ways to interact without too much fear.

We feel that that this is a crucial component. The psychology and the right practice of the right skills, which we think is having structured talks to deal with issues. We also think the focus should be on getting all the students working together to help each other get better results. This guy shows how kids can work without teachers, which means can you imagine if we changed how they were taught, maybe by getting them to explore in a structured way rather than being lectured to like we do now. We see some great food for thought to make some positive changes.

Self-education experiment.

(Scan the QR code or hold down Ctrl and click the link)

https://www.youtube.com/watch?v=dk60sYrU2RU

After we have a bit more of a chat, the rest of the group leave and it's just me and Steele, he has been staying until last after the sessions and usually walking me home. He is definitely growing on me and since we have been working on this together, I have not seen any of the old Steele come out. He seems to be a lot more respectful and although he still seems to have a sense of humour and jokes around a bit, it is not at the expense of anyone. In the past he would make comments about others, usually loud enough for them to hear and people would laugh, but the person it was about would literally drop their heads in embarrassment or shame and slink away. As you can appreciate, they would see him coming and disperse out of his eyeshot, but in class there was often nowhere to hide so he pretty much made comments about others and got his laughs at the expense of them.

He is definitely a different person than he was and it has been a few weeks now and there hasn't even been glimpses of the previous Steele. I have also been spending a lot of one on one time with him and find myself flirting a little and I'm pretty sure he is flirting with me, but I am conscious that he is trying to make up for Josh's death and I don't want to misread his interest in me as something romantic rather than wanting to do "right" by Josh, so once again I have this fear of trying to find out if he genuinely likes me or not.

I put that aside and we start to walk home. Steele is a little quieter than usual and so I feel a little uncomfortable with the awkward silence and start to make small talk, but he seems preoccupied in his mind, so I ask him what the matter is? The question distracts him and breaks his thoughts and he is suddenly back in the moment with me. He looks at me quite intently, which is not a look I had seen before. He then breaks eye contact with me and is intent on looking at something other than me. I start to feel a little bit funny in the tummy, but it's kind of exciting. He fleetingly looks back at me but then looks away again. I can see he is quite uncomfortable and I ask him, 'Are you going to ask me out?' I do this because I can see him grappling with this and I just want to help him out and I have been hoping he would.

He looks at me much more intently and asks if that is OK. I laugh and tell him absolutely that it's OK if that's what he is asking. He says yes, he would love to take me out, but he was worried how that would come across given Josh and all that has happened. I was ready to say yes, please let's go out, but him raising Josh makes me somewhat less excited as I rethink what brought us together and I suddenly feel sick and nowhere as euphoric as I was before. I'm a little bit worried about this suddenly and the cogs in my head start to go a bit nuts.

What if others think it's too soon and I am suddenly letting Josh down again by going out with the person who ultimately led to his suicide? All this goes through my head very quickly and I say I'm not ready for that. Inside I'm already beating myself up because I really want to say yes, but these thoughts overwhelm me and the memory of Josh. I hear another me say the words, 'I'm not ready for that.' I can see his disappointment and I choke down my own. I feel like I'm not myself as I say it and I can't describe the feeling, but it's not good.

We walk without talking for what feels like an eternity. I can see I have hurt his feelings and while we have that silence, I question my response and want to change my response, but all these factors I go through in my head. Would others really respond badly, would they think I have somehow sold out on Josh? Here is this guy I punched in the face and who is directly responsible for the suicide of Josh who I secretly had a mad crush on and a couple of months later I am prepared to go out with him. Oh shit this is worse than I thought! Can I ever really do it? I say to him that I'm not ready yet but I do like him but I need some time to think. He seems to perk up a little but I guess he knew this was a tougher question than if he asked someone else given the circumstances.

He walks me home and gives me a small kiss goodnight and my stomach does a backflip. I regret saying no to going out already, but the fact that he still kissed me heartens me. I'm trapped between doing what I think others will think is the right thing for Josh and what I actually want, but also my own thoughts about Josh. I really don't know what to think. I go into my room and start just checking stuff on the net.

I relook at the post from Will Smith about Fault and Responsibility, which resonates with me. I feel I need to take responsibility for myself and not blame others anymore. Even with my decision in a way I'm blaming Josh and blaming others for my own decision, and now I regret it already and just on something as simple as accepting an invitation to go out together. Yes, we factor in others views but ultimately, I know fear has been a big part of my decisions up until now and I really do want to see myself become a "leader" which is definitely not what I have been. I decide I need to take all this research and the information I have been exposed to, since Josh took his own life and walk the walk and actually do something for myself and then make sure I can influence others in a positive way too.

I start to think of Steele and I start listening to some cool songs: Macklemore: *Good Old Days:*

(Scan the QR code or hold down Ctrl and click the link)

https://www.youtube.com/watch?v=1yYV9-KoSUM

I especially like this one and it does make me think of Steele and I'm feeling energised. Ed Sheeran: *Perfect*:

https://www.youtube.com/watch?v=2Vv-BfVoq4g

I really want to take these leaps and challenges for myself. I am totally intent on stepping up to the plate and changing the person I was. I look back at where I was before and I really can't see myself going back to that person, who would "shrink" from view so that others wouldn't pick on me or my friends. It really is my time to take some control and as Will Smith said, 'Get outside of blame and take some responsibility.' I can almost hear Clint saying, 'Yes blame is a red brain response because you are looking back the whole time and can't move forward, but taking responsibility is looking forward and this evokes that blue brain response. You suddenly have options, whereas with blame you just stay in that same space, looking back!' I'm kind of excited and I am determined to step out of the shadows, no more shrinking for this young lady. I start thinking of how I want to shine and a few songs pop into my head, so I check them out.

Diamonds remix with Kanye.

(Scan the QR code or hold down Ctrl and click the link)

https://www.youtube.com/watch?v=KZSkVcvJnWk

Shine: Shannon Noll

https://www.youtube.com/watch?v=g09cKEkNwoU

I drift off to sleep feeling pretty positive and looking forward.

Chapter 48

The session with the group goes really well and we seem to be gelling as a group. I also have been thinking about Taylor a lot and really enjoying her company and she is very cute too, so my feelings for her are definitely growing. I'm ordinarily not very shy when it comes to girls, I haven't had too many issues asking girls out and usually get an idea that they might like me and can pick up whether they are flirting with me and then would ask them out and pretty much get a yes almost all the time. With Taylor, I'm actually worried about her response if I do ask her out. I have been playing it over in my head and analysing how she has been with me and I'm looking much more intently for signs that she is in to me, but its a little grey for me. I can't see anything concrete.

I start to walk her home and I'm trying to think straight because I'm torn between wanting to ask her out, but I'm not sure of her answer so there is a fear I'm going to embarrass myself and it will stuff up the friendship we have developed through this post-Joshua process. I keep weighing up the pros and cons for wanting to ask her out and I'm kind of distracted in my thoughts until she snaps me out of that train of thought when she asks me what is wrong.

I look at her briefly not really hearing what she said. I want to ask her out but the fear holds me back. She surprises me and asks if I want to ask her out. I feel a relief because now I'm thinking, *OK she does like me and I feel it's OK to ask her and she will say yes.* So I ask if that is OK. She laughs and tells me absolutely that it's OK if that's what I'm asking. I say yes, I would love to take her out, but I was worried how that would come across given Josh and all that has happened.

I can see this changes her own thoughts because I really think she was about to say yes, but now she is thinking about Josh. I secretly kick myself for bringing Josh up and changing her focus from a blue brain one to a red brain one. I can see how different these focuses make us look at things now that I have a deeper understanding of that. I realise I accidentally changed her focus and the "feelings" that comes with that are painful for her. She says she's not ready yet, but she does like me and needs time to think. I actually feel pretty good about that, because I now have some confirmation that she likes me and this really swells my chest and I realise I had just been in a red brain space only seconds ago, and how quickly it changed. I walk her home and give her a kiss on the cheek and she seems quite happy with that, so as much as I'm disappointed she said no, I actually feel pretty good with the overall outcome, plus I know with all that has happened she would be worrying about what others might say if she suddenly started going out with me, so I do understand that.

I go home and go through the discussions the group had that night. I look for ways that students can interact better and take into account more empathy for others and find something rather cool.

Naomi at school:

(Scan the QR code or hold down Ctrl and click the link)

https://www.facebook.com/bbcnews/videos/10155512752052217/

I find this idea of bringing a baby into school kind of cool and how they explain how much more vulnerable the baby is even compared to them and they understand how the baby needs to be cared for and it creates opportunities to discuss things, which is kind of the part we think is missing and ties in with the issue about young people on their phones and not actually not interacting. It has a lot of merit and can be something we should definitely look at "teaching" the kids.

I also find this from a guy who was let down and how he turned things around in his life. Again when you dig down, he was focusing forward in a blue brain space rather than looking back and again not focusing on whose fault it was. He literally tells the story like Will Smith said and took responsibility. He came up with his own solutions and that is how it all started. He was then able to keep gaining momentum and seeing improvements rather than sitting and blaming, he took charge. Control your own destiny:

(Scan the QR code or hold down Ctrl and click the link)

https://www.facebook.com/goalcast/videos/1753233504753832/

This one I also find on my search and it kind of pulls things together in my head, based on what Clint was saying, which was doing something small but different will lead to bigger things and improvements. Her making 5-second decisions created a different wiring and firing in her head and she saw more improvements, which gave her confidence and suddenly it became easier. It then started to grow more and more, because the new neurons in a positive manner were effectively wiring and firing together, and ultimately you have a more positive robust person not getting stuck in the negative pattern. Tiny decisions:

(Scan the QR code or hold down Ctrl and click the link)

https://www.facebook.com/goalcast/videos/1671299799613870/

I'm starting to feel confident with the material and starting to see a lot of similarities and trends or patterns that seem to be coming up repeatedly. I start to really think about what I did in my thoughts diary and how just thinking about my thoughts actually did have the impact Clint was talking about. The fact that he then told me to not only write them down but then analyse the ones that were toughest and "manipulate" them in my head, especially if they were repeat thoughts. He talked me through this manipulation, which was to talk to my unconscious brain like it was another person and tell it what to do with that thought. Such as telling it to stop right there, which allowed me to pause the thought in my head and then talk to how I wanted it to change or ask it questions of what this thought can teach me or what things I could do to make it have less of a negative impact on me and more of a positive effect instead.

The process was about interrupting the "autopilot" thought she mentions in this video and turning it into something else. In a lot of these videos it is all about interrupting this thought pattern and then doing something else and it really is about preventing those neurons from wiring and firing in the same way over and over until it is habitual. The interruption and then the changes mean we change the habit and in her case, she realised that it was about the "action" before the brain, the subconscious autopilot brain took over and led back to inaction. She was able to force through that and put in "good routines" as Clint keeps mentioning. The penny is certainly dropping for me, how important those good routines for us as young kids can be. I also see how the Naomi activity above allows those young students to do things they would never do and exposed them to routine or habits of wanting to care for another human who cannot take care of themselves and also cause them to interact and talk about the process and what they were learning with each other. I certainly don't recall ever really doing anything like that at primary school, talking about my feelings or empathy.

I see how this can help me and also help me help others, which I guess is what Josh really was after when he decided to send the DVDs and the letter to Clint. In a weird way he actually has helped me so much, I have sat with my own thoughts for a while since he passed and I realise I wasn't a very nice person and I do think about what type of person I would become had this not happened. If I'm honest with myself, I know that it wouldn't have been a person who really gave a rats about anyone else, the world would have revolved around me and I actually see that I could have become my father, who is very successful in business, but in reality his relationships and the way he contributes is not good and probably quite superficial.

I am also more excited now than ever about wanting to be with Taylor. She was someone I never noticed until now and I know I want someone "different" to who I was interested in before Josh died. I had been out with a number of different girls but they were all ones I chose who would be the ones others thought were the best looking or the most athletic, it was all about their looks and my ego. I would literally get bored after being out a couple of times, because it was all about wanting to be this stud that my friends would be envious of. I realise now how superficial I was and how deep-down underneath there was literally no fulfilment in it for me. I actually feel my stomach actually twist in embarrassment and shame as I think of myself only a few months ago and how others would have seen me back then. It's not a good feeling, but I also learnt a lot since then, so I catch that feeling and am determined to do things better and be the better Steele that would probably never come out if this didn't happen.

I'm not feeling tired and decide to explore more around depression and start looking on the net and my search finds a lot. Choice seems to come up in these things numerous times. The other common pattern I see is about overcoming fear and doing something else. For the woman talking about the 5-second decisions, she had her snap moment, where she realised she didn't want to be here (at this point, hitting the snooze button) and just that rocket countdown moment was enough to break the pattern, but she had to do it again and again, which she did and things started to budge and then more and more things started to unfold for her.

Depression ideas:

(Scan the QR code or hold down Ctrl and click the link)

https://www.youtube.com/watch?v=1I9ADpXbD6c

I like this one about really focusing on exercise, again it is forcing you to DO something and exercise does a couple of things, it is physical and emotional and you can see progress and it has that psychological change again. It actually motivates me to look at doing something. I laugh and can't get the idea of the NASA countdown out of my head as I wake to my alarm the next morning as I prepare for my first run since Josh died. I feel pretty good leaving while the air is still crisp and I feel the air moisture in my nostrils. I'm not running very quickly but I feel how hard I'm breathing and I'm actually feeling pretty unfit, but I also feel positive and strong within myself. I think of Taylor and the group and the work we are doing with Clint and I feel I'm in a truly good Blue Brain Space.

Chapter 49

I wake up feeling pretty energised, I'm kind of excited to let Steele know I have thought it over and frankly I do want to go out with him. I do still grapple with what others will think about that, but I am determined to do what is good for me and also, I know I'm not actually hurting anyone else. I think it through and wonder why we are so worried about other people's opinions, even though I get that we want others to like us, why do people get into such a spiral when people say negative things about them on Facebook, even when we don't know them at all. I figure from now on my attitude is actually "Blue YOU!" I could use a more rude 4-letter word, but that's not me and Blue seems appropriate given what we have been learning and discussing.

I text Steele to see if he wants to swing by my place and walk with me to school. He promptly replies he will be here in ten minutes. I smile inside and on the outside, I'm pretty excited and feel myself wanting to do cartwheels. The radio is on and a song I haven't heard for a while is on, it's nice and high energy and I'm singing along loudly mind you.

Neon Trees: *Animal*

(Scan the QR code or hold down Ctrl and click the link)

https://www.youtube.com/watch?v=gM7Hlg75Mlo&list=PLM4Rkj1rxQg6ew3RQmKqd_UaW3hoYuDAa&index=46

I quickly go outside as I see Steele approach as I'm watching for him to come into our street. I walk out and I am met by a well-groomed Steele, who clearly looks like he has made some extra effort and a very broad smile. He looks at me and seems to smile even more broadly, I find myself blushing, but it's him who breaks eye contact and seems a little shy which is very unusual. It actually makes me find him even cuter, because he seems uncomfortable and…a little more vulnerable which I hadn't really seen before. I say hi and he says the same. He walks up to me and I put my hand out for him to take and he does, as we start to walk side by side towards school. My belly is doing backflips and I can't contain myself anymore and blurt out that yes, I want to go out with him!

He stops and faces me and I can see excitement, but also relief on his face as he smiles at me. He doesn't say anything and proceeds to kiss me. This is different to the other kisses he has given me; he literally puts his hand under my chin and kisses me gently on the lips which literally does make me a little light headed and I open my eyes when he stops kissing me. He opens his eyes too and we both laugh at each other and he says he thought he was going to pass out as he was also feeling a little giddy. This makes me laugh a bit more and we walk to school hand in hand, both feeling like we are emitting some kind of light.

We know we are an hour early because Clint and Ben Gray wanted to meet with us and formalise what we want to do. We all come together and discuss all the things we have discussed and the things we know can help the students, the things teachers and the school should be doing along with what we can do. We give Clint and Ben all the ideas we have already tabled and indicate that we see this as their work to take on and make something a bit meaningful from an education perspective, but we had been talking about what we as students would like to do.

I tell them that would like to set up something to remember Josh, we would like to organise an event or concert to raise some money to help with suicide prevention, but we also say it's not enough to just make people aware of suicide, that we want to invite others to come up with ideas, tips, interventions, whatever it takes to help with not only child or youth suicide but to help males, females and any other human who is struggling with things in their life to get from HERE to THERE, whatever that HERE is, we want to help them get there.

We discuss what we want the event to look like and we all agree we want to organise a concert with as many of the artists that Clint has mentioned in this book to be able to sing the songs listed here to help with suicide prevention. We ask Clint, because it's his book what song he thinks is the most hopeful song he can think of and he comes up with a song we didn't actually know. He plays it for us and we all feel like it is a fitting end, the words are very hopeful and a little idealistic, but it works. Now the goal is to make this concert happen. Where do we start?

Somewhere in the World Tonight: Altiyan Childs.

(Scan the QR code or hold down Ctrl and click the link)

https://www.youtube.com/watch?v=G69YWb28ekc

Chapter 50

For the next few months, I worked closely with the school staff and students, and some other schools have also asked for my assistance. As I was working with them, I had been working on a bit of an instruction manual which summarises what is in the book and may give them some ideas and tips to help with resilience.

I ended up putting together the following program, which is the new Full Mental Jacket, it coincides with some of the videos I did a while ago. It is aimed at young teenagers and also educators and parents who may need some help.

The key for me on mental health, and reducing suicide from an educator's perspective, is to get them to understand self-leadership first and then doing things to help these students in that way. The following chapters are the contents of Full Mental Jacket.

This can be used separately from the previous chapters and is a stand alone guide. I hope you find them useful.

Chapter 50(a): Understanding Fear and Anger

Over the years, a combination of factors, including my studies in psychology and rehabilitation as well as my experience as a police officer, injury management consultant and HR professional has led me to the view that we do not teach our children key "vital behavioural skills". More specifically how to take control of our thoughts, because without doing that it can then lead to a significant number of issues later in life.

There are certain key behaviours which involve enhancing self-awareness, and how an individual then chooses to deal with situations as they arise. If parents and schools were more aware of the physiological and social psychology, they can certainly help them to grow up and deal with life in a much more robust way.

I am going to cover off some basic psychology for ease of explanation, but acknowledge that there is a greater complexity involved, which includes neurotransmitters and hormones etc., but in this context, we do not need to go to that detail.

I will focus broadly on two areas of the brain (see image below to show size differences)

1. The Cerebral Cortex (which I will refer to as BLUE BRAIN)
2. The Amygdala (which I will refer to as RED BRAIN)

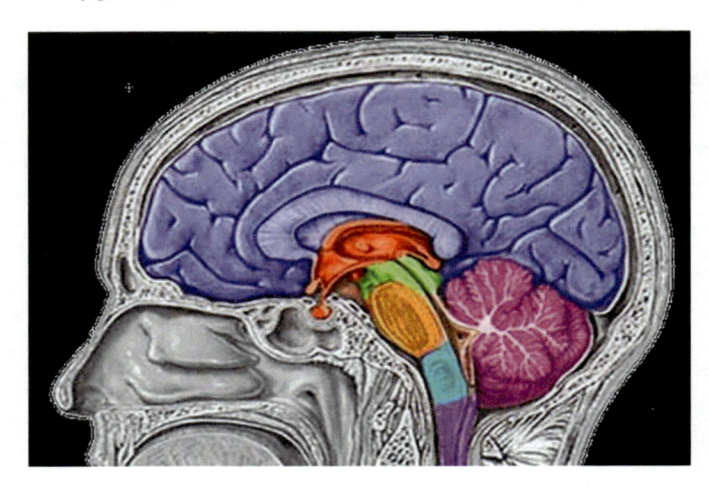

Blue Brain is quite a large part of the brain. It is:
- The reflective part of the brain.
- Linked to where we do our conscious thinking and analysing.
- It involves our imagination, creativity and labels our emotional state.

- The blue brain requires a lot of blood to function.

Red Brain on the other hand is:
- Linked with fear, the primary emotion and the secondary emotion, anger.
- Responsible for the emotional component of a memory.
- Activates body's response to danger.
- Involved in emotional learning.

Memories of emotional experiences are imprinted in synapses in this area.

In this instance I am going to focus on how fear and anger can have a negative effect on us. While the emotions themselves are not bad, they can be extremely limiting and dangerous if we allow it. As a police officer, I have seen many angry people who have done things in anger that have left their lives and others' destroyed because of their actions.

Fear is another component which can be limiting and dangerous. Fear at its extreme can lead to phobias and high levels of anxiety that prevent people from even venturing out of the house in some instances or have such irrational thoughts and worries it affects their lives in a very detrimental way.

As we grow up, this "fight or flight" instinct, Red Brain can become a big component of unconscious learning and this forms an undercurrent of the type of lens that we view the world through.

The way we are wired affects how we learn when we are young. It is important to understand that there are four parts involved in what we learn and how we make decisions over time in terms of what we have learned and "how" we have learnt them in the past.

The four components are the CUBE model (which I have changed from the initial CUPE model):

1. **C**onscious Thoughts (Blue Brain)
2. **U**nconscious Thoughts (Includes various parts of the Brain)
3. **B**ody (Physical)
4. **E**motions (Feeling/Physical)

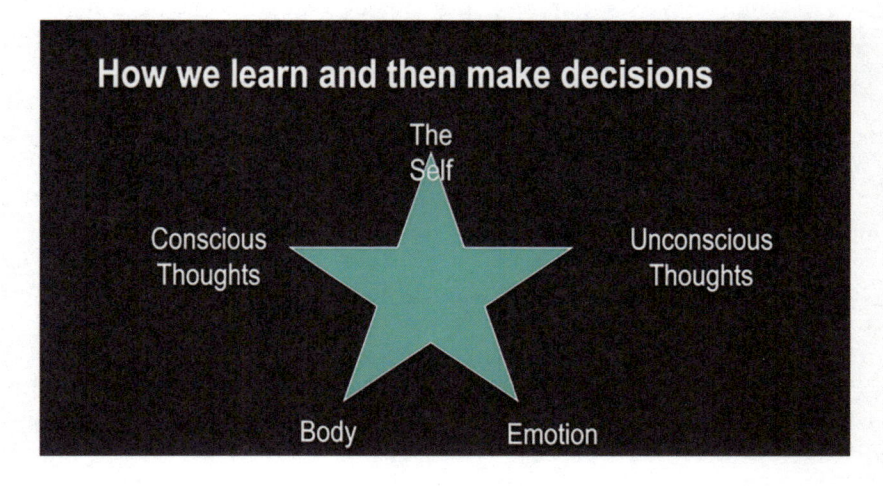

How we learn and then make decisions

The Self

Conscious Thoughts

Unconscious Thoughts

Body

Emotion

As a baby, most of what we take in is quite passive and because we are not able to "consciously" make sense of the world from our experiences and surroundings, we are mainly taking things in unconsciously, even the physical experiences although tangible, are processed on an unconscious level.

Young children don't yet have an analytical mind to edit and make sense of what happens to them, so most information they absorb comes in at a subconscious level. As children we are more highly suggestible so if something happens with high emotion, on a subconscious level we build a subconscious association with whatever caused that emotion, which is how early childhood experiences become subconscious states of being.

It is also important to understand what actually happens when we have a thought and how the body, brain and emotions all become involved. According to Dr Joe Dispenza in his book *You are the Placebo*, 'when we have a thought, the brain creates a neurotransmitter and it creates a neuropeptide which sends a message to the body, which reacts by having a "feeling". The brain then generates a thought matched to that exact feeling that will create chemical messages that allow you to think the way you were just feeling. As we complete this process for the first time as babies, we are greatly affected by what is happening around us.'

If you are unfortunate enough to be born in a violent or angry environment, you make sense of the world through the experiences you have, and you have thoughts and "feelings" that go with these experiences. This could invoke a fearful undercurrent or increase the chances of an aggressive one. Ultimately the more you repeat the pattern of thoughts, and go through the same process described above, it becomes hardwired and eventually the body subconsciously becomes conditioned to become its own mind or decision maker.

We have this view that we make decisions with our conscious and rational brain (blue brain) but in reality, we make it with how we "feel" and how it has been hardwired into our body through the experiences and emotions we have attached to it. How we react in situations is also dependent on the others around us. The social aspect of us as humans plays a huge part in our behaviour.

To illustrate, I would use the following example. If I fall over in front of my group of friends, they will laugh and tease me, and more than likely I will laugh too and probably not worry about it too much. But let's say the same thing happens in front of a girl or boy I really like or complete strangers? Suddenly the context is different even though the physical event is relatively the same. Now there might be an element of embarrassment or shame. This can turn into something if we "choose" it to, and many have allowed themselves to get stuck on an event in which they felt shame.

As we grow up and interact with others, we constantly get feedback on how we should behave, and we learn the rules of the society or culture that we live in. Often, we use fear and shame as a way to get people to comply. The laws of the land often have penalties associated with any breaking of those laws. This is intended to create a fear of punishment to create law-abiding citizens.

In a similar way at the family level, parents and other family members will also use fear and shame to get their children to be obedient and conform to what that society considers acceptable behaviour. This can be subtle but is intended to make the person fearful of being shamed. Comments about body image or not being good enough or wearing the wrong clothes from a parent can have lasting effects and the child has those thought patterns hardwired and feel an emotion associated with that thought in the body. When you really think about it, the motivation has a lot more to do with the parent and what others would think of them as a parent if the child was misbehaving. So their own fear of being shamed and being labelled a bad parent prompts this.

This is all quite unconsciously learnt, and the child will have their thoughts and behaviour shaped. This is also not a bad thing as we want our children to be accepted within society and follow the rules and become strong citizens that contribute to the world in meaningful ways, but sometimes the intention causes negative patterns. So, if someone is continually "feeling" fear, they can develop that undercurrent of fear and then they develop that fearful lens. Fear and anger do go hand in hand, as the survival instinct is either fight or flight, so over time some people instead of fear can develop an anger pattern, which plays out in them being bullies or just being aggressive as their undercurrent.

In my roles in HR I have come across patterns of behaviour that show the impact of this undercurrent of Red Brain. The Human Synergistics research gives some insight on this,

(Scan the QR code or hold down Ctrl and click the link)

https://human-synergistics.com.au/

as it compares managers across the world based on three styles, one, which is the constructive style (Blue) and the other 2, funny enough is based on an aggressive defensive style (Red) and a passive defensive style (Green). https://www.human-synergistics.com.au/about-us/the-circumplex

Those with high scores in these two styles tend to be less effective. Those with the aggressive styles in short have more people related issues, while those who are highly passive, and defensive tend to be highly compliant and people pleasers who tend to worry more and as managers can get trodden on.

So, what has all this have to do with helping with mental health and resilience, I hear you ask? I believe that the reason a lot of people don't ask for help if they are struggling with mental health issues is because there is a fear factor attached to them discussing the issue. Possibly the fear that they will be considered weak or of being laughed at or many other fears, but ultimately it is our home life and society that has instilled that "pattern" in us, so we don't talk about things in a good, constructive way.

The reason people don't raise issues at work is for the same reason. There is a fear factor with raising poor behaviour with a colleague. There are common factors in a lot of these social interactions, but it is actually the mental struggle and the understanding of this fear and anger and how it can dominate how we interact and how we can either choose to act or choose not to act. Making a decision to **not** do something is also an action.

Understanding fear and anger and how it shapes the individual, especially in a social context is the key to helping children to grow up into healthy, mentally and socially strong individuals. I will again refer to the four components that really make up a person:

- Conscious Thoughts (Blue Brain)
- Unconscious Thoughts
- Body (Physical)
- Emotions (Feeling/Physical)

If you think of the person in this context, most of our initial thoughts have been quite unconscious and the emotions, and how we feel is already hardwired into the body and taken place mostly unconsciously. Regardless of what is hardwired, the only way to make changes if fear or anger has been a dominant factor is to consciously think our way out of it ourselves. Parents and schools can help provide an environment and opportunities to develop better patterns of thought, which can then be hardwired and diminish the effect of fear and anger.

You don't drown by falling in the water, you drown by staying there!
Edwin Louis Cole

While I am mostly focusing on fear and anger, because it is a survival instinct and can have a significant impact on us, doing this work can also assist with others helping us deal with other emotions. As the quote above suggests, our emotions aren't bad, but being stuck in a consistent pattern of an emotion can be devastating. Sadness, shame, fear and anger can all have a negative impact if we let it.

My view on what skill is vitally important for schools to introduce and to provide regular opportunities for the children to practice is "crucial conversation" skills. The reason this is important is that if done well, it can allow the children to overcome any fears of having any type of conversation. Being able to address issues early on is extremely important to calibrate behaviour. It needs to be deliberate by the school in terms of what behaviour is expected and what will not be acceptable.

In the book *Crucial Conversations* by the team at Vitalsmarts, they introduce the Dialogue Model (below). In a nutshell when we have a conversation, we are throwing information into a pool for anyone listening. Each person sees or hears that, they tell themselves a story, they feel a certain way and then they act. If both parties are feeling comfortable (safe) in the conversation/dialogue, then they will continue to put information into the pool. But if there is some element of safety not being present, they can then go outside the pool and be in the red zone which takes them to silence or violence.

(Scan the QR code or hold down Ctrl and click the link)

http://raysxfit.blogspot.com/2011/06/conversations-tips-for-relationships.ht

Again, fight or flight comes into the equation. If the person goes to violence it ultimately ends up in an aggressive response by one of the people and then if the other person also responds that way, we have an argument, and no one is having a constructive conversation. If one of them goes to silence, they essentially "clam" up and won't say what they really mean. If you follow the sequence from See & Hear to Act, this is essentially based on that pattern of behaviour we have developed leading up to school.

As students start at school, teachers should be made aware of the dialogue model and how they help create the safety for the students to have conversations in the pool to address issues and focus on solutions. Essentially my suggestion would be to allocate specific time each day, preferably towards the end of the day for students to talk about things that happened to them, which they may not have been happy with, including someone else's behaviour. These should be facilitated by the teacher who is looking for anyone getting defensive or aggressive. The key here is to make it regular and get the students used to giving and receiving feedback.

Over time it gives them the skills to effectively talk about issues and it also allows much better calibration and feedback on each person's behaviour, because each student also hears what acceptable behaviour is and what isn't. It also allows the individual to hopefully stay calmer in those situations and develop less fear at the "Feel" phase before they act.

The other component for the teachers to understand is how they develop "courage" in their students. Setting up those conversation opportunities is helpful, but to accelerate the process and get them to overcome negative unconscious patterns they have developed before they got to school, they need to understand the importance of the "conscious thoughts".

Dr Joe Dispenza likens our unconscious thoughts to be like riding a wild horse. It can take us to great places, but if **we let it**, it can take us into bad places as well. He says that in order to get it to work for us, **we need to take control of it**. The only way to do that is through our conscious thoughts. As described earlier, you understand how our negative thought patterns can develop early on, but we can proactively develop good thought patterns as well and these get hardwired and become habitual as well. The key is around using our conscious thoughts to do this deliberately, especially if there are any habitual negative thoughts.

Through my work with people with PTSD it is evident we can obviously develop negative patterns of thought through a number of different ways, even from a single bad experience. The key again is to consciously do something to change it and then use that conscious thought pattern to develop plans to change the old habits into better ones. This helps to make them become hardwired, so that the "story" we tell ourselves is a more positive one and our feelings are better, which lead to better actions.

Chapter 50(b): The brain and counselling

In the last chapter, I covered what happens when we have a thought and how that thought leaves an impression on the body and how we create a lot of our thought patterns unconsciously. In this chapter, I really want to focus on how we break negative thought patterns once the person is already stuck rather than focus on preventative strategies.

There are obviously a number of ways we can end up with negative thought patterns and being stuck in those patterns. Some of these patterns can be mildly negative and others can be catastrophic for the individual and others around them. When someone is in that mindset where they are ruminating about the same thought or memory, they are essentially firing neurons in their brain because it is a thought.

In the previous chapter, I covered a small component of what happens in the body when we have a thought. I will take it a small step further, and again I'm trying to keep it simple, so any clinicians out there, I know there is more neuroscience and biology behind this. In a nutshell when we have a thought or recall a memory, we fire neurons in the brain. If we rethink that same thought or memory, we fire the same neurons. If we repeatedly rethink that thought or memory over and over, those same neurons fire together repeatedly. Dr Joe Dispenza in his book *You Are the Placebo*, states that in relation to neurons, 'What fires together wires together.'

In a nutshell if you do it enough times, you effectively create a "thought shortcut" and that thought is now almost automatic and requires a lot more effort to change than if it was not hardwired. Our brains are designed to be able to create shortcuts, so we can learn and then do things with less mental effort. To illustrate this, think back to when you learnt to drive, how hard you had to concentrate on what you were doing. You were thinking and concentrating on the road, your hands, your feet and the rules of the road. While you are learning to drive, you usually come home quite mentally drained. Fast forward to my age (48) and you have been driving over 30 years and you can drive for hours and are not even be aware of things, especially not the driving part, because our brains are cognitive misers.

We are designed to try to save energy and we create these shortcuts, which in essence is just a pattern of thinking. Most of the time this is a good thing for us, but when we set up shortcuts which can lead to destructive thought patterns, it can be a problem. When I worked with people with PTSD, where a single event had caused them to develop a destructive thought pattern, it was evident that by "reliving" a memory, that the body has quite similar physical reactions to the memory or thought, which is what makes it so destructive. Sometimes it's not even the memory but the realization of what could have happened, and that thought pattern dominates.

Let's say you were shot at, like one of the police officers I dealt with when doing counselling work. The event was very real and very scary for him and probably most of us. In that moment his "fight or flight" instinct kicked in and this started a cascade of events almost immediately and quite automatically with no conscious thought being required. That cascade involves adrenaline being released into the body, you take a deep breath to get quick oxygen into the body and your blood starts to be dispersed to your muscles to get ready to either run or fight. Your heart rate increases dramatically to distribute the blood quickly. There are some other physical components to this cascade, but this is designed to get you out of trouble quickly and avoid whatever threat is there.

In this officer's case it kept him alive because he ended up not being shot and was able to shut down the threat. End of story you think? Unfortunately for him, after the event and in the confines of his own head, he replayed the event over and over and basically he tricks his own brain into turning this thought into a shortcut because he has "practised" this thought repeatedly and the brain being the cognitive miser it is, turns it into a habit requiring less energy and accessing it a lot easier and quicker. To go with that, each time he has the thought it sets off the same physical cascade that is associated with the memory.

Dr Neil describes it this way:

(Scan the QR code or hold down Ctrl and click the link)

http://www.thebodysoulconnection.com/EducationCenter/fight.html

When our fight or flight response is activated, sequences of nerve cell firing occur and chemicals like adrenaline, noradrenaline and cortisol are released into our bloodstream. These patterns of nerve cells firing, and chemical release cause our body to undergo a series of very dramatic changes. Our respiratory rate increases. Blood is shunted away from our digestive tract and directed into our muscles and limbs, which require extra energy and fuel for running and fighting. Our pupils dilate. Our awareness intensifies. Our sight sharpens. Our impulses quicken. Our perception of pain diminishes. Our immune system mobilises with increased activation. We become prepared, physically and psychologically, for fight or flight. We scan and search our environment, "looking for the enemy". When our fight or flight system is activated, we tend to perceive everything in our environment as a possible threat to our survival. By its very nature, the fight or flight system bypasses our rational mind, where our more well-thought-out beliefs exist, and moves us into "attack" mode. This state of alert causes us to perceive almost everything in our world as a possible threat to our survival. As such, we tend to see everyone and everything as a possible enemy. Like airport security during a terrorist threat, we are on the lookout for every possible danger. We may overreact to the slightest comment. Our fear is exaggerated. Our thinking is distorted. We see everything through the filter of possible danger. We narrow our focus to those things that can harm us. Fear becomes the lens through which we see the world.

So back to my officer, every time he thinks about this memory it sets off that same cascade. This is only designed to last less than ten seconds, but when our thoughts make us relive the same event and create that shortcut, it has implications in terms of energy usage, the amount of hormones and other chemicals in the body like cortisol. These can be physically damaging to the body. Even just having the blood shunted from the digestive tract repeatedly means nutrients aren't going where they need to go. It is not hard to see visible signs of physical effects on someone who is going through this for prolonged periods.

When I am dealing with someone with PTSD, my focus is pretty much on what we can do to change the neurons that are wiring and firing together when the person has these thoughts or memories. Essentially, we are trying to initially interrupt the thought pattern and replace it with another. To simply illustrate, let's say 100 neurons (this is a made up figure for illustration purposes only) are fired when someone has the thought and it sets off the stress response and it leads them down a path that leads to them feeling shamed for reacting the way they did (this is what this officer did). With him I got him to first do a thoughts diary, where all he did was write down the time of day, he had that thought and write something about how it made him feel, with specific focuses on his physical feelings and sensations.

The purpose of this was to interrupt his previous pattern even just a little, so as an example maybe only 90 of the initial 100 neurons were firing, so it created some small change. As well as cutting the numbers of neurons firing, by making him do analysis work, it means he needs to use a different part of the brain (Blue Brain from my last chapter). This helps the interruption but because that part of the brain is so large, it requires more blood which also interrupts the fight or flight cascade, because he needs to send more blood to the brain rather than to his limbs, so it actually helps him at that physical level as well.

In just one week, he actually decreased the number of times he would enter having that thought in the diary, just by doing that analysis work. Naturally this doesn't work for everyone, but the point is that any intervention can work if it gets the person to somehow interrupt and/or change the repeated wiring and firing of those same neurons that takes the person to a bad place.

Even though I have studied psychology, I don't really have a preference for which type of psychology theory or therapy strategy is used, as long as it interrupts the neurons firing. This is why many strategies can work. Even talking to someone or doing something physical can help. Some people find religion and that works for them, because they have a Blue Brain focus rather than a Red one. Meditation also has a calming effect and actually slows the brain waves, which again is giving the person an opportunity to alter their original thought pathway.

The key for helping anyone in that kind of pattern is figuring out ways to get them to do **something,** anything to change those neurons and keep doing it with whatever helpful methods they can come up with. Asking them high level questions also forces that blue brain to think and come up with answers. Obviously sending them to a professional would help, but if they are not the type of person to seek that help, then do whatever you can. There are lots of things on the internet and various mental health organisations that give information on strategies that they have used and that you can try.

Also remember, from my previous chapters which includes the Dialogue Model, that to get someone to talk about these kind of issues is to create the "safety" to have that conversation. If someone doesn't want to talk about it, then there is something that makes them feel "unsafe" to have that conversation with you, so it is important to figure out what that is. Often it is them feeling shame for not being able to deal with the issue. Pointing out that this is quite a common problem may help them feel less shamed and then feel that you aren't going to judge them. There are various methods to try to create that safety and finding out what they may be afraid of in having that conversation is a key to getting them to open up and start talking about helping strategies.

Chapter 50(c): Creating resilience

As a parent I know most of us want the best for our children and we try to do things to shelter them from harm. But are we actually creating future adults who have very little resilience and are more likely to struggle with life and mental illness in the future? I personally think so.

In one of my previous chapters, I explained how we as humans learn and develop a lot of our "personality" or our "self" quite unconsciously and we are shaped by who we interact with in our very early years, which for most of us is our parents and the closest family members until that circle expands when we start school or pre-school. As I also pointed out before, in a lot of cultures we as parents and other influential people and institutions such as religions use fear as a strong influencer of our behaviour. This is mostly only a mild form of fear. They say things like, 'If you don't do what I want you to do, then…something negative will happen.' You could be grounded, miss out on dessert or some other punishment, which unfortunately does create some aspects of fear in the individual and if that happens a lot early on in life, then fear and aggression later can become an undercurrent of how you see the world.

Humans are social animals and so language and dialogue are key components to developing social relationships, but it can also cause a lot of pain and anguish. When I referred to the Dialogue Model (see below) in a previous chapter, I indicated the role fear and anger plays in conversations or dialogue we have with each other.

(Scan the QR code or hold down Ctrl and click the link)

http://raysxfit.blogspot.com/2011/06/conversations-tips-for-relationships.html

When we think of bullying at an early age at school, it's usually someone who is trying to dominate someone else and it can play out a number of ways from them teasing a person or saying negative things. Underneath it though, the bully often comes with that undercurrent of fear and acts out on it through aggression and wanting to dominate others. Often no one says anything to them, because they themselves are fearful to confront the bully, so nothing happens. Or if it happens to a boy, often the parents will tell their son to toughen up or not take it seriously.

We use the Dialogue Model to illustrate how these interactions play out. First you have the bully who is having the conversation from the Violence, red section, which is outside the Pool of Shared Meaning, where good helpful dialogue takes place. Now the child being bullied sees and hears what the bully says verbally and also sees their actions and facial expressions. They tell themselves a story, now dependent on what their undercurrent is, they too could go to Violence and verbally snap something back and suddenly you have an argument between two people in red brain, which is likely to escalate and certainly won't be enhancing the relationship they develop.

If the bullied child on the other hand is fearful of the bully, which is most likely as bullies tend to pick on less physical threats, they will try to go to the Silent side of the model, where they try to ignore being teased and just stay silent hoping it will go away. Others may be hearing this and sometimes laughing at the bullied child if the taunts are humorous. Both parties hear and see this, and this is how some bullying behaviour is actually facilitated by the group. The bully gets a dopamine reward because he or she is entertaining people and they have responded in a positive way to the behaviour.

The bullied on the other hand, sees people laughing at them and tells themselves another story. What do you think that story would be? Very likely not a good one for developing a healthy self-image. They could start to question whether the group likes them or accepts them or not. How they interpret this is now a crucial moment, because how it then makes the person feel and then act has the ability to have a long-lasting effect.

If, however, the bullied person learns the skills to stay in the Blue pool and in Blue Brain, through facilitated conversations this can be a calibration process for the group and the bully. If I was facilitating this, we would ask all the kids if anything happened today that they didn't feel good about. As the teacher or facilitator, it's about "creating safety" for the kids to say something. There are several ways to do it, but it is important that you are focusing on creating the safe place to have conversations from the students first day at school. The key is to make it routine and habitual to do it, so when asked, all the students get used to and comfortable to have these conversations and help them unpack some of the "fear" undercurrents they have formed.

Having these conversations daily and early on should help in a few ways.

1. The children calibrate behaviour with each other.
2. They feel less fearful having these conversations.
3. They become more skilled at having these conversations.
4. Hopefully if they deal with issues sooner, they can form better relationships with each other.

The thing about bullying behaviour is that it is dominance behaviour and once you understand this, then we can help our children deal with it a lot better. Below is an excellent link to a video that illustrates it better and quicker than I can put into words.

(Scan the QR code or hold down Ctrl and click the link)

https://www.youtube.com/watch?v=7oKjW1OIjuw

Although Brooks Gibbs is doing a role play here, in the first half as the bullied person he is exhibiting a combination of silence and violence responses to the bully, which shows some defensive comments and also some with a bit more of an aggressive tone. The second time around it is a calm person being careful with what they say and doing it in a way that could actually enhance conversation and that is where not having a fight or flight undercurrent is the key. If schools are deliberate about creating opportunities to reduce that undercurrent and set things up correctly, it can do a lot for the outcomes and the relationships they form.

It can help create resilience through habitual practice, also giving the children courage (really creating the safety is doing that) to have conversations about behaviour they don't like. This gives them that sense of having some control and is good for their personal development. The more they talk in that context, the more they are likely to talk outside the classroom as many have not formed poor relationships because the issues are dealt with before they become issues.

Naturally this is just some small strategy to begin with, but it is vitally important that it starts being considered for use at school level and as early as possible. A lot comes back to which neurons are wired and fired together. We want the thought patterns being developed to be more positive and schools and parents can do more if they know what is happening in the children's heads and how they can facilitate structured interactions better.

Chapter 50(d): The inner story.

In the previous three chapters, I covered on Red Brain/Blue Brain and understanding how fear and anger affects the undercurrent of us as a person. I covered how the body, unconscious and conscious thoughts along with our emotions pretty much makes up the "self". While I did also cover the dialogue model and how we think when we have conversations, I think it is important to focus now on how we can create patterns of thoughts by our inner dialogue.

In the Dialogue Model there is the step after **See and Hear Something**, which is **You tell yourself a story**. The story you tell yourself will determine the next step which is **Feel**. Then based on how we "Feel" will determine how we **Act** or in some instances don't act.

(Scan the QR code or hold down Ctrl and click the link)

http://agilecoffee.com/toolkit/crucial-conversations/

Our interactions with others and the relationships we form and avoid are determined by this. The see and hear part is really out of our control. People can do and say nasty and hurtful things to us, but the rest is actually within our control. The story we tell ourselves when we are very young is based on the undercurrent and habit-forming thought patterns we have developed mostly on an unconscious level, but then as we come into contact with others more and more often, we bring this pattern with us and it affects our interactions and relationships with those people.

We will never be friends with every person we meet, and we will have some biases, beliefs and views on the world that will differ with others, but the internal story we can shape in a way that works for us rather than one that hurts us. If my internal dialogue was *"that bad things always happen to me"* or *"that I know I'm not good enough"* then how I feel is likely to be negative and this affects how I Act. In the Dialogue Model if I come into contact with someone and they seem confident and I am having this kind of internal dialogue where I don't feel good about myself, it's very likely I am going to be more on the "silence" side and won't really want to interact. Some people from the outside might say I was "shy" but I could just be too scared to interact, so I will avoid those interactions and ultimately, I am then less likely to form good relationships with those people. Fast forward to high school and now I could be the outcast who has never really made any good friends because I don't put myself in a position where I feel comfortable interacting with a wide mix of people.

One thing we all need is to be accepted. No one wants to be rejected, so we dress a certain way, we talk a certain way and we usually interact with people who are more like us, so we can feel part of the group. Note, sometimes personal and socioeconomic factors means you can't wear or buy what you would like and this can be shameful. We are "creating safety" in the Dialogue Model by doing a mental risk assessment of our interactions and weighing up whether there is a chance of rejection if I even go and talk to that good-looking girl or guy? That undercurrent, the habits you have formed, and any hint of fear will have a direct effect on what story you tell yourself and then how you feel and act.

This is why it is so important for us to be helping our children and young adults with understanding this process and also how we learn and sometimes how to "unlearn" habits to help us thrive. Tony Robbins said in one of his seminars that basically the human body will replace every cell in the body within a couple of years, so we actually aren't the same people we were two years ago, but we maintain memories and can still relive painful episodes in our life, because we have developed habits that reinvent the "self" we have developed. Dr Joe Dispenza explains how we need to break the habit of being ourselves, by thinking differently.

The key is to do things differently and for young children, it's up to parents and schools to provide the opportunities to develop skills, knowledge and relationships in a better way, before those habits become negative. For adults, it's about understanding why they have certain thought patterns and working out strategies to break that wiring and firing together of those neurons and then creating different neural connections. It really is about being aware of your thought patterns and filling your head with as much knowledge of techniques or strategies that can help you think in a different way. Even just changing the scenery by doing a nature walk or playing golf can help break patterns of negative thoughts, but as Joe says, it needs to be body and mind. It is way more effective to be focusing on both if you are having negative thoughts or are feeling depressed.

Teachers could help calibrate early on in schools that not everyone can afford to buy certain things and help them to look past the superficial things.

Chapter 50(e): Creating Safety.

Each human experience is unique, even identical twins don't have exactly the same path. However, there are general patterns of how we psychologically deal with certain situations.

Many years ago, I read John Douglas' book Mindhunter. He was the FBI agent who was probably the father of serial killer profiling. In the book he covers certain risk factors that with some degree of certainty was what the killer would have experienced in their childhood.

These included being most likely to be a male and usually had a single parent and that parent was most likely the mother and that mother would usually be extremely strict on the child. She more than likely also shamed and humiliated that child. That child would then act out violently towards animals because they weren't able to defend themselves against the mother.

There are obviously many other factors that ultimately lead someone to want to kill multiple people. But the point is there are risk factors that can lead to a lot of our mental health issues. The key is to try to limit the risk factors, but at the same time we need to try to include as many of the success factors as we can and include those in our schools and at home.

That said, not every child has a loving home or can be protected from bad things happening. Life simply is not fair and so when someone does end up depressed or suffering from mental health issues, it is important that we utilise a number of strategies that help address those thought patterns that has brought them to that point.

Just medicating someone is not enough because it does not address the root causes. There are various therapies, theories and strategies and I am not aligned specifically to one. I am of the view that different ones can work for different people, but the key is to get the person talking about it or at least be looking for ways to improve their situation. When someone gives up then it is a much more difficult, if not an impossible prospect.

There is a lot more awareness initiatives such as RUOK day, but we need to address creating the safety to initiate these conversations with those we think could be at risk.

We actually need to show more courage to have those conversations. As I have stated in previous chapters, we need to develop that skill in our children, but we as adults too often feel fear of offending our friends, brothers and sisters by bringing up our genuine concerns. We need to take a look at ourselves and genuinely ask if we are worried about someone.

My view is better to do something than do nothing and then live with that regret. Courage comes in many forms but ultimately it is doing something when there is a feeling of fear when doing it. Suspecting a friend is at risk of suicide is a tough subject to bring up. So sometimes we simply accept when someone says they are okay but often it requires deeper conversations to get them to talk at that level.

Here are a couple of basic strategies you can ask them to do to make you feel more comfortable that they aren't hiding what is really going on. I mentioned a thoughts diary in a previous chapter and highly suggest this as a starting point. You must emphasise that they need to be honest with themselves while doing the diary for seven days.

All they need to do is carry a pen and notebook with them and record the date and time when they have what they think is a negative thought about anything and put a single line about the thoughts subject.

That is all they need to do. The purpose is to get them to do analysis work which uses a different part of the brain and this can help breaking previous thought patterns. It also shows how much negative thoughts are popping into their heads and gives great insight about the content of their thoughts.

Next step is to ask them questions about what they saw in the thoughts diary and if there were any aha moments. Asking them these questions does a couple of things.
1. It gets them to reflect again and this is a Blue Brain experience which keeps Red Brain at bay.
2. It shows you care and this enhances developing the safety for them to open up more. This is what they mean when they say develop rapport. The only difference is I'm giving you ways to do it.

From there it is important to keep asking questions like a coach would ask them what they can do rather than offer advice which we all like to give. Unfortunately, if they feel any hint of judgement, then it invokes a defensive response which takes them back to Silence or Violence in the Dialogue Model.

Chapter 50(f): You are the Director.

When I was doing injury management work with people suffering from PTSD, I could really see how an event they experience can affect someone in such a negative way, which is understandable. However, when it gets tricky is when you see how the memory of that event continues to have that effect on the person and as I previously mentioned, that thought pattern can be disastrous.

When I was doing counselling sessions with these individuals, it was important to get them to acknowledge that what they initially experienced was something real, and that can't change, but the way they "manage" that event or memory of that event is the key. I get them thinking about the event as they remember it, but I get them to think of the memory as a movie scene and they are the director, so they can make changes to it as they see fit.

The intent was to get those different neurons wiring and firing together and making small changes to the pattern of thoughts they have been stuck on. We then discuss what they could have done differently or better or maybe change the scenery a little or even include a different character. Basically, anything to change those neurons helps, and this is done by changing the focus, even get them to put a funny spin on it, make changes to it as the director would. Why, I hear you ask…because they can. We can think our way out of these thought patterns.

Once we understand how this process works to get us into negative patterns of thought, we can focus on the same process to get us into better patterns of thought. This is why habits or addictions like smoking are best beaten by replacing it with something else while someone tries to give up. It alters the person's focus from not having the cigarette and what thoughts that brings up, to focusing on something new, which does alter the wiring and firing of the initial reaction.

In the counselling sessions, I would get them to "practice" being the director and alter the memory of that event as many times as they could as homework between sessions. On top of that I would ask them to think about what they wanted at the end of the therapy. I would get them to focus on a future state, which as you now know is a Blue Brain experience for them.

Getting them to practice the changing of the memory does a couple of things, it shows them they have more control over the memory and their own thoughts. It also shows them that it is actually themselves that is causing the issues they are experiencing. By starting with the end in mind, they also have a goal and it changes their focus. What they focus on is what they get more of. If they continued to focus on the memory of the event, it would have continued to be an issue until they did something to break that wiring and firing of the same neurons every time they had that thought.

Chapter 50(g): Directing our children.

In the previous chapter, I covered how I would help my clients in counselling by becoming a director of their own thoughts and thought patterns to help them get out of patterns that were doing them harm.

In my view we can use a similar approach, but a more structured and proactive one to help our children as they are developing. It is obviously important for parents to understand the basics of what has been covered in the previous instalments. With some of that knowledge they really can help prevent some negative patterns from forming, and with better knowledge they can actually focus on how they and their children can direct the thoughts they want to form.

Understanding how a child develops thoughts and how it is hardwired into patterns, which form moods, then personalities and beliefs. We can actively put good thought habits in place by questioning them better around how they feel and what they are thinking.

The key on this is them knowing they have conscious control over how they react even when things don't go their way. I think a lot of parents don't have these kinds of discussions and they don't give much thought to "planning" what they would like their children to learn from them, so it just happens by osmosis and we hope they turn out okay.

I recently went to my 30-year school reunion, so it has been a while since I was in school other than my tertiary studies, but I don't recall anyone really teaching us anything about how we think and how we become the people we end up being.

In my police days and my HR roles I have seen so much wasted potential in so many people who are stuck and it plays out in them being bitter and quite nasty people to be around. They have poor relationships at work and at home and they generally make others around them miserable too.

Structural coupling is when someone comes in the room and either brings energy or takes it away from others in the room. We need to help our children to not end up being the energy takers. There are certain skills that can help with dealing with problems. As Dr Stebbins says in his book the *Stress Surfer*, if you have a problem you can do something about, then it requires problem solving but if it's something you can't do anything about then it requires coping skills.

Knowing how you learn and think and feeling comfortable to have conversations and asking for help when you are feeling down are important skills, we should be teaching children at home and in schools. As parents and educators, we should be actively looking at the research and consistently look at life skills as well as the rest of the curriculum. Long-term studies should be used to try to find what strategies may impact on creating more resilient, more confident and capable adults for the future.

Examples like the Stanford Marshmallow experiment conducted in the 70s where young children were offered a marshmallow, but if they delayed eating it for a certain period, they could get a second one. In a nutshell they found years later that those who were able to delay the gratification of eating the marshmallow the longest, appeared to be more successful at life in general and they had much higher activity in the pre-frontal cortex, which correlates with the Blue Brain activity I covered in a previous chapter.

The point being that there are some skills and strategies we can explore further and look at influencing the children at an earlier age in a structured way, while we consider how they learn how they interact and how they develop relationships.
Below is a link which explains the Stanford Marshmallow experiment.

(Scan the QR code or hold down Ctrl and click the link)

https://en.wikipedia.org/wiki/Stanford_marshmallow_experiment

Chapter 50(h): Shame and Guilt

When we think about how we learn and are taught to fit in with others, we can see how sometimes those methods can be destructive, because ultimately, we have an "inner voice" which is largely unconscious and non-verbal, so it comes out in how we "feel". I have covered in previous chapters how we think, learn and make decisions with our body a lot more based on how we feel and not use our "logical" brain like we might expect we do.

In a previous chapter I covered how we often use "fear" (usually of punishment) to get citizens and family members to comply with certain rules for a number of reasons. In various societies over many generations we use shame, humiliation and guilt to teach people to conform, fit in and become compliant citizens. In Japan, death is considered better than shaming your family. This is instilled in a growing child as they are taught the rules of that society and rightly or wrongly, they have a high suicide rate as a result.

Let's cover off on guilt and shame very briefly. One of the easiest explained definitions I can recall is this: shame equals to "I am bad". While guilt equals to "I did something bad". The reason these emotions exist is ultimately to help us fit in and develop relationships. Guilt in particular, is linked to our interpersonal relationships and as we grow up, we are calibrating to know and understand what is acceptable behaviour and what is not acceptable behaviour? This shapes what we say or do and also what we don't say or do.

When we think of how we learn to feel guilty, it is based on where we live and the key influencers in our lives, especially in our early childhood. The notion of "I did something bad" comes from those key influencers giving feedback, sometimes verbal sometimes through punishment, and this shapes some behaviour that we wouldn't do again because of the fear of that reaction. We learn a lot of rules along the way. Ever hear, 'Children should be seen and not heard?' These are ways we are shaped to behave. We are told that you can't always tell someone the truth, because we don't want to offend them. In Australian and British culture, we are taught to be polite, to have manners and not be rude. In other cultures, they may not be taught this politeness and then when people have different rules that they grew up with, it can create issues when we expect someone to act a certain way and they don't and vice versa.

This chapter is not about these societal differences but to illustrate how the society we are brought up in and the parents or early caregivers you are exposed to can have lasting effects on how guilt and shame can shape our lives. Shame, guilt and embarrassment are all quite closely related, and it usually involves the presence of others, it is there for the social aspects of our lives and mostly in a healthy way to be able to fit in and develop meaningful relationships with others. It can however also start a downward spiral if the person is not able to deal with deep shame.

In previous chapters I write about getting stuck in negative thought patterns and if we get stuck in a pattern of shame, we start to convince ourselves and tell ourselves, "I am bad". This type of thought pattern can be destructive because unlike, "I did something bad" we can easily believe that we can't change being bad and we can start to feel worthless. If we get picked on about our clothes for example, and people laugh at us and humiliate us in front of others, we start to look at ourselves as worthless and not up to where others are, and our internal dialogue comes back into play. Those "unconscious thoughts" quickly turn into internal dialogue that reinforces that we are useless, and we start to listen to the internal dialogue.

When you feel shamed and humiliated, it is difficult to share that experience with anyone because generally you are feeling ashamed and telling anyone can make you feel more ashamed, so most people internalise it and keep it silent. After a while they can feel ashamed of feeling ashamed, which creates even further internal dialogue and with social media these days other people can send stuff online to humiliate you even further. If the person is already vulnerable, then it can lead to destructive behaviour including suicide.

Often with people struggling with certain mental health issues, their reactions can make them feel more shamed and this can worsen their condition such as depression. I worked with a police officer suffering from PTSD and he was more concerned with how humiliated he felt because he was crying a lot because of the PTSD and this was not what he saw as what was expected from him as a man and as a police officer. He found that thought much worse to deal with because in his head it questioned the persona of himself that he identified himself with.

To help him with this, a lot of work was done on getting him to realise that he was experiencing an illness like any physical one which affected the way he was feeling and the way he was thinking. I don't mean to compare mental illness with having a bad cold, but to illustrate a point, when you have a bad cold where the physical symptoms are a sore throat, runny nose, coughing etc., this all affects our general mood and we don't feel that great and in this case physical symptoms leads to some psychological distress and with mental health it can do the same. The key is calling on resilience and being able to work through it using strategies that slowly break those thought patterns and change the neurons that fire and wire together.

As parents it is important to really think about how we reprimand and teach our children and it is important to focus on nurturing them in positive ways. Barbara Fredrickson at the University of North Carolina has found that positive emotions, like trust, curiosity, confidence and inspiration broaden the mind and help us build psychological, social and physical skills. While there will be times where the old methods of raising your child by using punishment will be used, it is important that we think about how we use shame and humiliation.

This has ramifications for schools as well. I did my primary school years in South Africa and the teachers would put up everyone's results in order highest to lowest. I was lucky I was a reasonably good student and now that I reflect back, it would have been extremely humiliating for those who had not done so well. It would be bad enough that you didn't do well but then to have it made public, it can't be that helpful. I guess the rationale is to "motivate" them to do better, but ultimately in that type of scenario there will always be people at the bottom of that list and it is important to think differently to change some of this.

Why don't schools promote each class as being a team and getting each one of their students to want to help their classmates and develop each other. It can be explained that just like a sporting team, say in cricket not everyone is great at batting or bowling or fielding, but we can all do our bit and contribute to the team. High performing teams learn from each other, work together push each other and also develop good psychological safety. This helps so they can talk to each other and have good conversations and dialogue about each other's behaviour in a constructive way rather than one that makes someone feel ashamed. If it is structured in such a way that students learn to do this well and actually are taught, they aren't against each other that their whole class and the school would benefit from them all doing well, then it's a massive win/win. But, we must resist the urge to give everyone a ribbon for turning up, because life is not fair, and they will need to deal with some disappointment while also developing overall resilience.

I honestly believe that if you have less structural components at school and at home that would result in shame and humiliation then that can only be a positive thing. If you received feedback done in the right way with the right intent even if it is negative, the person can start to get that calibration with their peers and get a much better understanding of what is "healthy" interaction and then dialogue can also develop, which increases those relationships.

If children can have opportunities to raise issues daily about anyone else's behaviour in their classes and it is facilitated well by the teachers, it helps build their confidence, increases that calibration and improves relationships, which is a great outcome. If teachers then implemented strategies that also foster team work from them all, where they would focus on helping each other, this also helps relationships build and develops a less selfish culture. Long term this means that they have support from the class and teacher and they are developing skills that make them more resilient and less likely to "shy" away from crucial conversations when they are required.

As mentioned above, throw in some strategies which foster positive emotions, like trust, curiosity, confidence and inspiration to broaden the mind. This will help us build psychological, social and physical skills then we are on a much stronger road to developing intelligent, socially good and highly resilient people who actually work as a team and take care of each other. I would like to think this would lead to less health (physical and psychological) issues, better school retention and ideally less criminal activity and reduced suicide.

Chapter 50(i): Breaking the Pattern.

In order to break the pattern of repeated negative thoughts, we must stop the neurons in our brains from wiring and firing together in the same way. There are many different ways to do this, but it is important to understand that when we have a thought, certain neurons fire and when we repeat that thought the same neurons fire. When they repeatedly fire over and over, then these neurons wire together and create a "shortcut" which means it becomes easier and easier to fire together. This is how we create habits and is why habits can be difficult to break.

As children we can unconsciously create thought patterns that we don't even realise. We create thought patterns that we consider to be our personality. Someone very shy or highly anxious may have an underlying thought pattern which they developed which involves an undercurrent associated with fear, of embarrassment or humiliation. This may have stemmed from the parents and became a habitual thought pattern, now they look at the world from that point of view and when they are in social situations, they "feel" uneasy. They then avoid those situations and this process keeps repeating itself and the same neurons wire and fire together when they are in that situation. Even anticipation of the potential of that situation becomes a trigger.

A single event can also create a pattern of thought. This is how PTSD can come about, where a person can experience an extreme event and the memory of that event becomes what they focus on. They will replay that event over and over in their heads and again the same neurons wire and fire together until they can automatically think of the same memory. They can also ruminate over what might have happened and this process, if repeated multiple times, can trigger the same fight or flight responses which can be destructive.

The key to "breaking" that cycle is to change the neurons firing that have wired together. There are many ways to do that. I mentioned using a thoughts diary in a previous chapter, which helps interrupt the thought continuing like it normally would, as it forces the person to use the analytical part of the brain, so it forces more blood back up into the brain rather than into the muscles to get ready for fight or flight. Over time I usually get them to add layers to that activity, so instead of just recording whether they had a negative or positive thought I get them to describe the thought a bit more, again the purpose is to reduce the times of those same neurons firing and wiring together.

The next step is to then start "doing" something else when they catch themselves having those thoughts, so I get them to practice an activity. It can be anything really, but I use a "centring" activity. They have to stop and think about their posture, so they must focus on trying to lengthen their body by standing up straight, head as high as it can go, pin the shoulders back so they open their chest and then focus on deep slow breaths for ten seconds. This again uses different neurons and helps interrupt the wiring and firing of the destructive thought pattern. Naturally they can do some other activity, but ideally, we want to do something that makes them stop, think and then do something else. It is good to have them develop a positive thought and physical habit which they can use at any time that the negative thoughts pop into their heads.

In a previous chapter I write about being the director of your own thoughts. With PTSD I also get the person to "freeze frame" the thoughts and play around with the thought in their heads and make some changes to it. This process causes them to not just interrupt the thought, but it forces them to use the imaginative side of the brain, which steers them away from any fight or flight amygdala generated thoughts. It also forces the blood again to pump back up into this large portion of the brain away from the muscles.

Another way they can break the cycle is to think of their unconscious as a character or person. I tell them to give it a name, something friendly. I call mine LJ and I will have conscious internal dialogue where I consciously tell it what I want it to do and what I don't want it to do. A few years back I would have horrible mental images just pop into my head at random times and it would set off a fear response, where the hairs on the back of my neck or arms would stand up. In this case I started to really talk to LJ that I didn't want those thoughts to come in. I would do that every time it happened for a couple of weeks and I noticed slowly but surely it got less and less and now it hardly happens.

If we can think our way into situations, we can definitely think our way out of them. The key is to understand how thoughts work and how they cause us to "feel". Once we know how thoughts work and how habits and thought patterns form, we can reverse engineer them to work for us in a more positive way. There is certainly a strong push for a "positive psychology" approach and while I think it is a good place to start, sometimes you can't just think positively, you actually need to deal with the habitual thought first by making changes as I suggested above and this can slowly be replaced with more positive psychology including affirmations.

Another technique to help someone going through tough thought patterns is to get them to do something for someone else, like volunteering. This again is what I call a Blue Brain experience because it causes them to focus outside of themselves rather than focus on the internal negative thoughts and negative feelings it brings with it. Once you focus on wanting to help others, it activates the frontal cortex which is associated with the social aspects of us as humans, which again helps with the interruptions.

Also doing something physical and changing scenery are all other strategies to help with this process. Mindfulness and meditation are other techniques which helps change our focus and replace it with something more positive. This also changes our brain waves, which helps with relaxing and slowing things down. There are many ways to make these changes, but if you know how you think and what these strategies need to do to be effective, which is to stop the wiring and firing of those neurons and replace with something else, then you will be more likely to get results.

Chapter 50(j): Taking Control

In the previous chapters I explained how we passively take information in when we are very young and how our thoughts and body intertwine to create a "feeling". I also covered patterns of thought and gave some strategies on how to break these patterns by doing certain things that stop certain neurons wiring and firing together. All those things are important, but the most important is when someone has the intent to change what is happening to them. The saying goes, 'We get more of what we focus on.' So, if that is true why do we "choose" to focus on the negative? Sure, the unconscious is always scanning for anything that could be a threat and if it detects even a hint of it, then it starts our fight or flight response. But when there is no visible threat and the threat is in our thoughts, then you would think we could easily choose to not focus on the negative. Unfortunately, we don't and when we start that red brain response and it makes us feel fearful or ashamed or sad, we can get addicted to the chemicals that these responses illicit, especially if we have formed a habit of this type of thinking. This then brings repeated physical responses and that is how we can crave the response even though it is not good for us.

No matter how you look at it, destructive thought patterns create destructive physical responses, and this can lead to very dark places in the person's head. The keys are focus and intent. Firstly, if we are not constantly focusing on the negative things happening, then we already can change which parts of the brain are being activated. That is why focusing on something like gratitude can help. By focusing on something or someone that you are grateful for, means you are focusing on something good and when we think of those things, it does not stimulate the amygdala, it activates different parts of the brain. Being intent on where you focus becomes a key first step to moving from a dark place.

The reason things like the book, *The Secret* and goal setting works is because it is about intent. Once you decide you don't want to be in that dark place, the focus needs to be to the future, because looking to the future uses that positive blue brain psychology and keeps you from focusing on the fear, sadness or anxiety. In my last chapter, I wrote about naming and talking to your unconscious mind, in this instance when you have intent and you know what you want to happen, you can start to control that unconscious mind by planning what you want the end game to be. Once you decide to change things, you can focus on setting goals for yourself and put together an action plan. The action plan needs to be activities based on helping with the changes, like the thoughts diary, or exercise, or volunteering to help someone else. They all need to be based around reducing the current destructive thought pattern and replacing it with healthier activities and thoughts. It is important to not be using excessive drugs or alcohol, which only band aid the problem.

Taking control is easier than we might think. When you know where you want to go, and you plan for it and you put together that action plan, the key is to then start the activities and use the activities to interrupt when the bad thoughts come. Slowly but surely things will start to change. You will notice less negative thoughts in that thoughts diary and they will last less and less. Just like the destructive thoughts can form a pattern, so can the positive thoughts, we just need to practice them in a deliberate way. Remember you get more of what you focus on, so focus on the things you want to come into your life. Again, you can plan for those things and put actions in place to make things happen. You really are the driver of your thoughts.

One of the hardest things to deal with, is the death of someone close to you. Nothing will ever replace that person and it is best to have a time to grieve and then celebrate the life they lived and the time you got to spend with them, which is why they are close to you. However, in this instance again it is important to try to focus on the future and ask your unconscious some questions that are positively framed, as it pushes the focus to a positive space. Questions like, 'What would that person want me to do with my life?' If that person was close to you, they would want the best for you and to go on and do great things, not feel sorry for them to the point that you don't take care of yourself or refuse to leave the house.

We are all human and bad things will happen in our lives, that is guaranteed. We will all get sad, feel scared and have various other emotions that come with being human, but we can dust ourselves off and move forward with intent no matter what life throws at us. Make sure you also keep in contact with friends and family because we can all help each other get through tough times. I'm hopeful these points can be used, to get us thinking of how we can help each other more, be involved more and just try different things, because there are many ways to the top of the mountain, try things, something just might work for you.

Another person doing excellent work on this stuff is Dr Hayley Watson, check out her website for ideas and real examples of young people getting through tough times.

(Scan the QR code or hold down Ctrl and click the link)

https://openparachuteschools.com/